MODEST

Men and Women Clothed in the Gospel

R W Glenn, Tim Challies
Cruciform Press | Released August, 2012

For the brothers and sisters of
Redeemer Bible Church and
Grace Fellowship Church,
lovers of the gospel.
– R W Glenn, Tim Challies

CruciformPress

"It is so refreshing to have a book on modesty that is a useful resource and not a legalistic, culture-bound list that leaves you a bit paranoid and guilty. No, this book is different. Its counsel on modesty is not rooted in rules, but in the grace of the gospel of Jesus Christ. That grace alone is able to get at the heart of the problem of modesty, which *is* the heart. In a culture where immodesty is the accepted norm, Glenn and Challies have given us help that every Christian desperately needs."

Paul David Tripp, pastor, conference speaker, and author

"How short is too short? How tight is too tight? Glenn and Challies don't say. But they do provide a thoughtful framework to help us come to a grace-based, gospel-grounded understanding of modesty that extends beyond mere clothing. They uphold a vision for modesty that's both beautiful and desirable—and not only for gals, but for guys too! This book is a great tool to help you wrestle with the practical question of what and what not to wear."

Mary A. Kassian, author, *Girls Gone Wise*

"The authors of *Modest* break new ground in their treatment of this difficult subject. It is a healthy antidote to the prevailing views, which tend toward either legalism or antinomianism, by grounding the whole subject in the gospel. I heartily recommend this book."

Jerry Bridges, author, *The Pursuit of Holiness*

"As a Christian who lives in a diverse global city [Dubai], I need this book. Every day I make conscious decisions regarding modesty as well as commit unintentional cultural *faux pas*. What does the gospel have to say about these things? I need the love of Christ to shape how I think about modesty in all of life; it's not just about bikinis and burqas. *Modest* is wonderfully edifying, encouraging, and practical."

Gloria Furman, author, *Glimpses of Grace: Applying the Gospel in Your Home* (Crossway, 2013)

Table of Contents

Cruciform Press

something new in Christian publishing

Our Books: Short. Clear. Concise. Helpful. Inspiring. Gospel-focused. *Print; 3 ebook formats.*

Consistent Prices: Every book costs the same.

Subscription Options: Print books or ebooks delivered to you on a set schedule, at a discount. Or buy print books or ebooks individually.

Pre-paid or Recurring Subscriptions
Print Book . . . . $6.49 each
Ebook . . . . $3.99 each

Non-Subscription Sales
1-5 Print Books . . . . $8.45 each
6-50 Print Books . . . . $7.45 each
More than 50 Print Books . . . . $6.45 each
Single Ebooks (bit.ly/CPebks) . . . . $5.45 each

Modest: Men and Women Clothed in the Gospel

Print / PDF ISBN: 978-1-936760-57-2
ePub ISBN: 978-1-936760-59-6
Mobipocket ISBN: 978-1-936760-58-9

One
WHY TWO GUYS WROTE A BOOK ON MODESTY

Uh oh — another book on modesty. And look, here's a surprise . . . it's written by men.

If that's what you're thinking, we want to assure you that this book will be different. We promise.

Discussing modesty among Christians is challenging because the subject typically has not been handled very well. Experience has trained us to expect a certain focus and vocabulary. We know that words like "spaghetti straps" and "bikinis" will quickly become part of the conversation. Maybe even "head coverings." And when a man is the speaker or the author or the discussion leader, women brace themselves, fearing an assault on their fashion sense and wondering if they are about to be blamed for all male struggles with sexual lust. *Does he think I have to be ugly to be godly?*

We know this is a problem. We've read those books, heard those sermons, attended those small groups, and reviewed those pamphlets. We are just as perplexed and frustrated as you are.

That's why we knew from the start that this book had to be different. In the pages that follow, we will not focus on your wardrobe. There's a sense in which we don't even care about your wardrobe. But we do care a great deal about your heart—whether you are a man or a woman. We want to see your heart so gripped by the gospel of grace that modesty becomes beautiful and desirable to you, not just in your wardrobe but in all of life. We want you to understand that modesty isn't just *motivated* by the gospel, it's an *entailment* of the gospel—it flows naturally from a solid grasp of the good news of the gospel.

Through a long history of unbiblical applications based in misunderstanding of key Scripture passages, modesty has been made into a kind of captivity, but we want you to embrace modesty as the freedom and delight God intends it to be. We wrote this book not because we have a bone to pick with women or because bathing suits make us nervous but because we want to help men and women both discover the joy and freedom of gospel modesty in all of life.

That's the short answer to the question about why two *guys* would write a book on modesty. For the remainder of this chapter we hope to explain why *anyone* would write a book on modesty. While we could marshal lots of reasons, we will give you just four:

- Because modesty has been largely neglected in the church.
- Because as pastors, we want to help draw constructive attention to the subject of modesty.
- Because the church desperately needs an understanding of modesty that is grounded in the gospel.
- Because the church needs an understanding of modesty that extends beyond mere clothing.

The Neglect of Modesty

How many Christian books have you read on the subject of modesty? Probably not many. Maybe not even one. Or if you have read something on the topic, it's likely been a pamphlet or booklet featuring charts and graphs and diagrams and checklists and lots of those dark red prohibition symbols X-ing out unacceptable items of clothing. In fact, it may be that very few people actually "discover" a book on modesty. Our guess is that most of those kinds of books are quietly slipped into mailboxes or handed to people with a mumbled, "You should really read this … really." Really.

Why is it that Christians aren't more clear and forthright about addressing modesty in the church? Partly because we have all had so many negative experiences surrounding the subject that we tend to shy away from it—there are too many charged emotions. But it's also because we have become desensitized to modesty as a culture. Modesty is seen as the rough equivalent of prudishness, and who wants to be a prude? Our culture is naked and brash and boastful and unashamed, and when you see enough skin and hear enough bragging, it all turns into white noise.

In a culture of immodesty, immodesty becomes normal.

Of course, this doesn't mean that Christians have lost the capacity to discern the modest from the immodest. We still have God's Word and Spirit, so although it may be difficult, immodesty is not impossible to spot. Unfortunately, when we do spot it, especially among our brothers and sisters in the Christian family, we can be sheepish about saying anything because we know how poorly the issue has often been handled. As a result, the whole concept of modesty drifts into disuse. It becomes a functional taboo—something you just don't talk about.

Well, we want to talk about it. And we want to talk about it in a way that's truly helpful and encouraging. We want you to be able to identify immodesty when you see it, but to do so *equipped with the desire and ability to restore, strengthen, and encourage one another in the gospel.*

Yes, modesty *includes* a woman's clothing choices, but it is *about* far more than that. We want to look at modesty in its full biblical scope, which means

- We must address the immodest *man* as much as we do the immodest *woman*, and
- We must address the person who *speaks or behaves* immodestly as much as the person who *dresses* immodestly.

All of that to say that the first reason we wrote this book is the sheer neglect of modesty.

We Are Pastors

Both of us live in places where the weather changes with the seasons (if you weren't aware, neither Minneapolis nor Toronto is trapped in eternal winter). Because of this, the issue of modesty comes up every spring, especially for women, and especially in relation to clothing. We can't tell you how many times we've been asked by the members of our congregations to address the issue. Interestingly enough, it's usually married women who are looking for help—not help for themselves, but help for the women in the church whose clothing choices honestly lack fabric. Their number-one concern is that their husbands will be led into sin because of another woman's allegedly immodest dress. We've yet to have anyone come to us and say, "Can you teach me about modesty? I have a lot of problems in that area."

It is difficult to address an issue when the problem is always someone else's.

Moreover, as we've already said, we know that modesty isn't an exclusively female concept. Many of the men in our congregations (including us two men) struggle to be modest in various ways. If we are going to care for our sheep, male *and* female, in their dress and in their character, we must equip them for a modest life. Therefore, we see this book as a function of our pastoral care — as a means of expressing love to the people we have been charged to care for.

So the second reason for writing this book is a pastoral one. We want to be better equipped to feed and lead the people in our care. Maybe you can benefit too.

Gospel-Centered Modesty

Even though modesty is a legitimate virtue outside of a Christian context, a distinctly *Christian* modesty must be rooted in the gospel of grace. That means we are also writing this book to show you how the gospel ought to inform and determine the parameters and motives of our modesty.

Far too often, guidance on this topic among Christians is rule-based: "This is godly; that is not. You must dress like this and not like that." But Paul pretty much shot down that entire approach when he told the church at Colossae to pay more attention to the heart than to rules about external behavior:

> If with Christ you died to the elemental spirits of the world, why, as if you were still alive in the world, do you submit to regulations—"Do not handle, Do not taste, Do not touch" (referring to things that all perish as they are used)— according to human precepts and teachings? These have indeed an appearance of wisdom in promoting self-made religion and asceticism and severity to the body, but they are of no value in stopping the indulgence of the flesh. (Colossians 2:20–23)

When we build theology without clear reference to the gospel, we begin to take refuge in rules. Perhaps our motives are good—we want to obey God and do what honors him—but even if the motive is sound, the solution can be wrong. The Christians in Colossae wanted to please God, and they wanted their faith to affect everything they did, but they ended up reducing their thinking about food and festivals to a list of rules: "Do not handle, Do not taste, Do not touch."

We aren't a whole lot better off today. When it comes to modesty we define the term too narrowly (our first mistake) and then surround ourselves with rules like "only this low," "at least this long," "never in this combination," and "never so tight that _____ shows." In fairly short order, the gospel is replaced with regulations. Indeed, in this particular area, the regulations become our gospel—a gospel of bondage rather than freedom.

The truth we are missing in all this mess is that *the gospel of grace informs and gives shape to what it means to be modest.*

Modesty without the gospel is prudishness. Modesty divorced from the gospel becomes the supposed benchmark of Christian maturity—perhaps especially for women—and a perch of self-righteous superiority from which to look down on others who "just don't get it." You may find yourself exclaiming disbelief about someone else's wardrobe: "Can't she see what she is (not) wearing?"

Modesty, apart from the gospel, becomes a self-made religion that can give some appearance of being the genuine article but that is in the end of *no value* (none!) in our battle with the sinful and inordinate desires of our hearts. If we reduce modesty to certain rules of dress, we are completely separating the concept of modesty from the person and work of Jesus Christ. As a result, we may have the appearance of godliness, but not a whole lot more.

So the most fundamental reason we're writing this book is a gospel reason. We need to be sure that our understanding of modesty flows from the gospel and leads to gospel love. If it doesn't, we've missed the mark and our modesty is no virtue at all.

What's Next

So there you have it. Three reasons why we wrote this book: because modesty is a neglected field of Christian study, because modesty is a pastoral concern, and most importantly, because we cannot let Christian modesty fall into moralism. It is and must remain one of the many outcroppings of the gospel of grace. For these reasons, we hope that you will continue to read this book. Our prayer is that as you do so you will be helped, encouraged, and challenged. Ultimately, we hope that you will find yourself reveling in the gospel of grace.

Two
DEFINING MODESTY

Definitions are important. If you don't know what you're talking about, you probably don't know what you're talking about. And when it comes to modesty, defining it is a lot harder than meets the eye.

The New Shorter Oxford English Dictionary has three entries to express current usage for *modesty*:

1. Having a moderate or humble estimate of one's own abilities or merits; unassuming, diffident, bashful; not bold or forward. "Leonard sat in *modest* silence, with lowered eyes."
2. Decorous in manner and conduct; scrupulously avoiding impropriety or indecency; reserved in sexual matters. "There was nothing *modest* or delicate in her approach to sex."
3. Not excessive, not exaggerated, moderate; undistinguished on the social or economic scale. "These were *modest*, achievable tasks."

Which definition should we embrace? When it comes to the English language, *modest* has a fairly broad range. It moves from something like being unassuming to being undistinguished. This movement alone can make defining modesty a bit of a struggle, but perhaps we wouldn't be too far from the mark to suggest that when we talk about modesty, we're talking about something roughly equivalent to Sense 2: "Decorous [proper, polite, formal] in manner and conduct; scrupulously avoiding impropriety or indecency."

The Bible itself leads us in the same direction. In 1 Timothy 2:9, a text we'll come back to shortly, the apostle Paul says "that women should adorn themselves in respectable apparel, with modesty and self-control." The word *modesty* translates a Greek term that appears only here in the New Testament. It refers to the quality of modesty, and it implies that practicing modesty gets you a kind of respect.

That doesn't add much to the English dictionary definition, does it? Especially since Greek dictionaries simply use the word *modest* again to translate the Greek underlying 1 Timothy 2:9. This text tells us that we should practice modesty, but it still doesn't tell us exactly what modesty is. We must think about modesty in ways that are practical rather than theoretical, and that should bring us greater clarity.

The Situational Context

To get practical, let's take something routinely addressed in discussions about modesty. How about bathing suits—especially women's bathing suits. We might think this would be a pretty easy one to lock down. And we have seen pamphlets giving all kinds of rules for what would be appropriate and inappropriate attire for the lake or the pool or the beach.

Let's say that we could agree on a one-piece bathing suit as modest. Not a two-piece in disguise; but a *bona fide* one-piece women's bathing suit. Is this modest? Suppose you said yes. Very well, then, if you're a woman, wear your one-piece to church next Sunday. Would you think it modest then? Would you feel comfortable at your church fellowship time holding a cup of coffee and your Bible while wearing your one-piece? My guess is probably not. You'd probably feel the need to cover yourself. And so would most of the people around you.

This illustration brings up one of the most difficult aspects of the subject of modesty—it seems largely like a contextual question. A one-piece woman's bathing suit may be modest, but not in an absolute sense. If it *is* modest, it is modest *for a bathing suit*, but probably not modest as an alternative to what you would normally wear to a worship service. In other words, what is modest or immodest is often a question of *situational* context—what is appropriate for one occasion may be wholly inappropriate for another.

The Cultural Context

Modesty is also a question of *cultural* context. A given society at a given place in a given time determines what dress and behavior are considered modest or immodest. Again, we go to 1 Timothy 2 for an excellent example of this: "women should adorn themselves in respectable apparel, with modesty and self-control, not with braided hair and gold or pearls or costly attire, but with what is proper for women who profess godliness—with good works" (vv 9–10).

We see clearly here that modesty and discretion are virtues (inner characteristics), but our culture determines the way that modesty and discretion express themselves in our dress and behavior (outward appearance). Apparently, wearing braided hair and gold or pearls or costly garments smacked of immodesty and indiscretion in Paul's time, but very few (if any) would argue today that braided hair is immodest and out of place in the church.

Can you imagine the scene? You come into church with your hair in a French braid, only to be taken aside by two older women who tell you that you need to "Dump the braid. It's immodest." You'd think you landed on a different planet! All this is to say that while all thoughtful Christians would agree that modesty is a gospel virtue, they would also agree that the expression of that modesty differs from culture to culture.

In our contexts, we have found that the most common "culprits" of alleged immodesty are beautiful women. The pretty girls take the most heat. But looking good isn't necessarily being immodest. It's just looking good. And there is absolutely nothing wrong with women being beautiful or even *making* themselves beautiful. To the contrary, God is the creator of beauty, and he delights in it.

What the apostle Paul condemns in 1 Timothy 2:9–10 is not beauty or adornment *per se* but ostentatious adornment—the kind of adornment that struts its stuff so as to call attention to itself. Sometimes Christians think that plainness is next to godliness, as if the plainer you look the more spiritual you are. This is rife with error, not least because many women whom the Bible commends for exceptional *inner* beauty were also known for exceptional *outer* beauty. Sarah, Rebekah, Rachel, and Abigail, among others, are all described as beautiful in form and appearance (see Genesis 12:11, 14; 24:16; 29:17; 1 Samuel 25:3).

Clearly, it is not a sin to be beautiful, and to display beauty is not in itself the sin of immodesty. Perhaps the beautiful women in our churches can be immodest and indiscreet from time to time—

but others in the congregation can also dress up their envy in the guise of someone else's alleged immodesty.

Confusing Modesty with Chastity

Finally, modesty is commonly confused with a related virtue: sexual purity, or chastity. C. S. Lewis writes brilliantly on this subject in *Mere Christianity*:

> The Christian rule of chastity must not be confused with the social rule of "modesty" (in one sense of that word); i.e. propriety, or decency. The social rule of propriety lays down how much of the human body should be displayed and what subjects can be referred to, and in what words, according to the customs of a given social circle. Thus, while the rule of chastity is the same for all Christians at all times, the rule of propriety changes. A girl in the Pacific islands wearing hardly any clothes and a Victorian lady completely covered in clothes might both be equally "modest," proper, or decent, according to the standards of their own societies: and both, for all we could tell by their dress, might be equally chaste (or unchaste). . . . When people break the rule of propriety current in their own time and place, if they do so in order to excite lust

in themselves or others, then they are offending against chastity. But if they break it through ignorance or carelessness they are guilty only of bad manners. When, as often happens, they break it defiantly in order to shock or embarrass others, they are not necessarily being unchaste, but they are being uncharitable.[1]

Lewis identifies common points of confusion between chastity (sexual purity) and modesty, and he brings us closer to a sound definition of modesty.

1. Lewis defines modesty as a "social rule." This harmonizes well with the Bible's understanding of modesty, as our brief foray into 1 Timothy 2:9–10 has made clear.
2. Because modesty is a social rule rather than a fixed absolute, it will necessarily change from era to era and culture to culture, and that's okay.
3. Lewis correctly implies that modesty is an issue of the heart. Therefore, the question in any particular instance is *why* a person has broken the rule of modesty current to his or her own time and place. To focus on the heart like this is the essence of gospel spirituality — what Jesus is always after.[2] There are only two possible reasons for immodesty: ignorance (where you simply did not know that you were being

immodest and therefore have not sinned) or dis-
obedience (where you did know, but just didn't
care).

4. In the end, chastity is about charity, or grace-
filled love toward others. When people are
immodest in order to excite lust in themselves
or others, or to shock or embarrass others, they
cross the line from immodesty into other sins—
sins like sexual impurity and a lack of love. Lewis'
clarity in this regard is especially helpful for us
because *our reaction to immodesty is more often a
reaction to the fruit of a certain kind of immodesty*
rather than to the immodesty itself. If we can
get clear on what is really happening in a given
situation, two good things result: we can be more
helpful to those who apparently struggle with
immodesty, and we can be more certain about
what exactly we may find offensive and why.

Now can we get closer to a definition of
modesty?

We see again—we can't say this too often—that
modesty is *not* what you wear or say or do. Instead,
modesty has three component parts:

- **Virtue.** Modesty is first and foremost a *virtue*—
an *inner attitude* that may be internalized and
largely unconscious, or very intentional.

- **Respect.** This virtue is grounded in *respect* for an *appropriate cultural standard* (the broader, general context) and *appropriate situational standards* (the narrower, specific contexts).
- **Result.** This respect is ultimately made evident in dress, speech, and behavior that willingly conforms to these standards.

We sum it up this way:

Modesty is that virtue which is respectful of a culture's rules for appropriate and inappropriate dress, speech, and behavior in a given situation.

When There Is No Such Thing as Appropriate

Now, if you live in the West, this definition probably raises an immediate question in you: what if your culture has no rules for appropriate and inappropriate dress, speech, or behavior? What if the whole idea of standards and appropriateness is up for grabs? What happens to our modesty then?

We have three suggestions: look carefully for the unwritten rules, remember the distinction between modesty and chastity, and be patient.

Look carefully for the rules. While there is some truth to the contention that our culture doesn't have a functional category for what is appropriate, it's not the *whole* truth. The example of the one-piece bathing suit is a case in point. If you wore it to a job interview, there's little doubt that your prospective employer would think you had dressed inappropriately (and, very possibly, that you are certifiable). So even if the categories of appropriateness and inappropriateness are a bit elastic in our culture, their elasticity doesn't mean that no such categories exist. Look for the rules. They might be harder to spot, but not impossible.

Remember the distinction between modesty and chastity. Take the thong bathing suit, for example. Apparently, there are some contexts—such as the beaches of Miami, Florida—where these are deemed culturally appropriate. While there, you're unlikely to find anyone looking at you askance for wearing your thong bikini on the beach. But cultural appropriateness is not necessarily the last word. We would argue that, even though in that context the thong bikini does not offend against modesty, it does offend against chastity. This is because the thong bikini has a primary aim that hits the target every time: arousing men. And arousing a man who is not your husband is always wrong. It might not be immodest, but modesty is not the only virtue.

Exercise patience. Our culture is in flux, and that makes this matter of discerning modesty a tricky business. It may not be that our culture has jettisoned modesty altogether as much as the changing tastes and contexts have made it harder to discern what is modest from what is not. C. S. Lewis is again helpful here:

> I do not think that a very strict or fussy standard of propriety [i.e., modesty] is any proof of chastity or any help to it, and I therefore regard the great relaxation and simplifying of the rule which has taken place in my own lifetime as a good thing. At its present stage, however, it has this inconvenience, that people of different ages and different types do not all acknowledge the same standard, and we hardly know where we are. While this confusion lasts I think that old, or old-fashioned, people should be very careful not to assume that young or "emancipated" people are corrupt whenever they are (by the old standard) improper; and, in return, that young people should not call their elders prudes or puritans because they do not easily adopt the new standard. A real desire to believe all the good you can of others and to make others as comfortable as you can will solve most of the problems.[3]

In other words, you may be disturbed by our culture's apparent jettisoning of the virtue of modesty simply because you have embraced an earlier (or different) standard that you then uncharitably demand that other people live up to. Lewis' advice is sound: "A real desire to believe all the good you can of others and to make others as comfortable as you can will solve most of the problems."

And this is the platform from which we want to do the heavy lifting of commending to you a gospel-centered approach to modesty. As the apostle Paul told Timothy, "The aim of our charge is love that issues from a pure heart and a good conscience and a sincere faith" (1 Timothy 1:5). Love is the goal— love of God and love of neighbor. Even immodest neighbors. No, especially immodest neighbors.

Three
PUTTING THE GOSPEL BACK IN MODESTY

The foremost reason we've written this book is that it's so easy to talk about modesty (or any other virtue, for that matter) without reference to the gospel.

Deeply committed Jews and sincere practicing Muslims, for example, find the immodesty of North American culture horrifying. But we're not interested in Jewish modesty, as good as that might be; neither are we interested in Muslim modesty. We're not interested in modesty as espoused by psychologists and sociologists who have observed the deleterious effects of immodesty on the psyches of young women. Nor is this book concerned with the negative things our immodesty communicates about what our society values. All of those observations might be interesting and even helpful to contemplate in another context, but we're primarily interested in the gospel—the gospel that has implications for all of life, the full-orbed right-where-you-live gospel. What we're interested in is *gospel* modesty.

Getting Clear on the Gospel

Obviously, we must be clear on the gospel if we will make any progress on something called *gospel modesty*. Just to be sure we understand the shorthand, we are using *the gospel* to refer to the centerpiece of the Christian faith and message, what Martin Luther called the article of faith upon which Christianity rises or falls—namely, the doctrine of justification by grace alone through faith alone in Christ alone.

What marks people who believe the gospel as uniquely Christian is not our modesty. It may seem odd to point that out, but the fact is that we often think of Christianity as a style or culture rather than as a faith that transcends both style *and* culture. We are marked as Christian—children of the heavenly Father—because he has justified and adopted us as his own, freely as a gift of his grace. As we'll see, this does not mean Christians are free to be *immodest*. But it also means that there is no such thing as "Christian" dress. There is only dress. If you turn the Christian faith into wearing one kind of clothing instead of another, you have added something to the gospel. But a Christian is simply a person who has come to understand and experience the grace of God through the gospel. Period. Modest dress does not a Christian make.

At the same time, the gospel of grace is not without demand. There is an edge to grace. And it looks like this:

> For the grace of God has appeared, bringing salvation for all people, training us to renounce ungodliness and worldly passions, and to live self-controlled, upright, and godly lives in the present age, waiting for our blessed hope, the appearing of the glory of our great God and Savior Christ Jesus, who gave himself for us to redeem us from all lawlessness and to purify for himself a people for his own possession who are zealous for good works. (Titus 2:11–14)

Precisely because God is full of grace, he is not content to let us continue in attitudes or behaviors that are not good for us. The grace of God doesn't cease after bringing salvation—it goes on to instruct us to live a certain way. This is where the edge comes in: grace makes us deny ungodliness and worldly desires because we should live sensibly, righteously, and godly. God cares about how we live, which means that he cares about modesty.

We might put it like this: God's grace *gets involved*. It gets involved in every aspect of our lives. There is nothing that God is not interested in changing for the better by his grace.

So on the one hand, the gospel reminds us that what makes us Christian is that God in his grace has justified us. He has declared us "not guilty" in his courtroom because Jesus lived the life we could never live and died the death we deserved to die—in our place. "Contrary to their merit and indeed in defiance of their demerit,"[4] the Lord accepts sinners freely, fully, and everlastingly! Contrary to your modesty and in defiance of your immodesty, you are accepted freely, fully, and everlastingly in Christ!

But again, on the other hand, that free, full, everlasting acceptance has implications. Grace makes an investment in every nook and cranny of our lives so that we may live to maximize the glory of God's grace in the world. Your skirt and shirt and pants and shoes (we're addressing both genders) matter to God!

Gospel Counterfeits

At this point, it is important to recognize that crouching right at the door of our belief in the gospel of grace are two gospel counterfeits—alternative ways of thinking that are ever-eager to move in and take center stage, thus directing our attention away from the gospel. The church father Tertullian described those alternatives with an illustration from Jesus' crucifixion. He said, "Just as Jesus was crucified between two thieves, so this gospel is ever crucified between two errors." The errors he was talking about are the ones *we're* talking about: antinomianism and legalism.

Antinomianism. Let's start with the bigger word, which is an idea less familiar to Christians generally. If you take the word apart, you'll understand it better: *anti* means against and *nomianism* refers to a certain approach to law. Theologians use *antinomianism* to refer to the fact that sometimes Christians turn grace into a license to sin. The short book of Jude acknowledges that grace has this risky aspect when it describes false teachers "who turn the grace of our God into licentiousness" (Jude 4, NASB). In the book of Romans, the apostle Paul addresses the issue head-on when he asks, "What shall we say then? Are we to continue in sin that grace may abound? By no means!" (Romans 6:1–2)

The idea is that we can look at how free grace is and twist it to mean that our thoughts, attitudes, and behaviors don't matter to God—as if it doesn't matter how we live because we're forgiven. Along with Paul, let us say "Never!" In supposing that sin isn't that big a deal, antinomianism forgets that there's an edge to grace. Antinomianism says, "It doesn't matter whether you're modest."

Legalism. The opposite of antinomianism is legalism. Legalists operate from the assumption that the Christian faith is performance-based. It's the mentality described by the apostle Paul in Colossians 2: people make rules "according to human precepts and teachings," but these rules only promote "an appearance of wisdom" and are finally "of no value in stopping the indulgence of the flesh" (vv 21–23). Many Christians, however, are consumed with exactly that kind of outward conformity to rules when it comes to modesty.

Legalism says that our acceptance by God is based on our own record, resume, assets, and accomplishments. Although it rightly understands that there's an edge to Christianity, it forgets that the call to live a holy life is not the *root* of the Christian faith but its *fruit*. Functionally, legalism seeks to avoid Jesus entirely. It says, "I can live up to the standards that God has set for me, and where I fail, I only need a boost from an all-but-superfluous Jesus." Legalism says, "Modesty *does* matter," but it says that for all the wrong reasons.

Now what is interesting (and so subtle) is that even though legalism and antinomianism look like polar opposites on the outside, they're identical on the inside. Both are "thieves of the gospel,"[5] as Tim Keller has put it: antinomianism steals from the gospel by twisting the grace of God into license to do whatever you want while legalism steals from the gospel by twisting the edginess of grace into law. And both look for ways to get out from under the shadow of the cross. Both try to avoid Jesus as Lord *and* Savior. Antinomianism avoids Jesus by resisting his lordship. Legalism avoids Jesus by rejecting his saviorship.

This is why we must keep the gospel front and center when it comes to modesty. *The moment we begin to consider modesty—or any moral, ethical, or behavioral issue—apart from the gospel—our thinking will inevitably drift toward legalism or antinomianism.* There is no other option. Either we explicitly acknowledge that we are entirely under grace with an edge, or we behave as though we are essentially under law. At that point, we will:

1. Reject moral guidelines (antinomianism);
2. Self-righteously embrace moral guidelines (legalism);
3. Ricochet madly between the two; or
4. Live with a hypocritical, inconsistent, illogical, and unfruitful blending of both legalism and antinomianism.

That last outcome is the most common. All Christians have spent at least some time in one or more of these categories, but we generally live in a blend of both views. Many of us live in that blend nearly constantly. And the only cure is to return to the cross—to remember the gospel.

When the Gospel Rules

That Jesus *had* to die for our immodesty should be sufficient to show how awful it really is. That Jesus *chose* to die for our immodesty should be sufficient to show how loved we really are—in spite of and in defiance of our immodesty. Properly understood, the gospel leaves no room for legalism or antinomianism. There is only grace with an edge.

So, then, how might we put the gospel back in our modesty? We have seen that modesty is part of biblical ethics, but we need to practice modesty with grace.

Antinomians see adherence to social conventions as a straightjacket. They say, "The gospel gives us freedom to dress the way we want. Our behavior doesn't matter to God. He looks on the heart." Meanwhile, legalists see adherence to social conventions as "the right thing to do." And the reason they do the "right thing" is that deep down they believe that doing it puts God in their debt. Legalists are not motivated to emphasize modesty out of gratitude for the fact that God has accepted them by sheer grace. Instead, what motivates them is the false sense of superiority they can have over the immodest, or the imagined sense of acceptance they can feel with God for their modesty.

But when the gospel controls your modesty, everything changes. You want to be modest because God sent his son, Jesus, to *die* for your immodesty and especially because Jesus *willingly* died for it. When the gospel controls your modesty, you won't see it as a way of putting God in your debt because you don't need to twist God's arm to accept you—he already accepts you freely and fully in Jesus Christ. This gives you both the ability and the desire to respond to him by joyfully being modest in appearance and character.

Four
WHERE THE GOSPEL AND MODESTY INTERSECT

In the previous two chapters we sought to define modesty and then place it in the proper context of the gospel of God's grace. This should help us understand that there can be no true modesty without the gospel. However, understanding and practice are very different things. The two come together at the level of the heart.

Without question, the foremost intersection of the gospel and modesty is your heart. If your heart is not fundamentally gripped by the grace of God as revealed in the gospel, then all your efforts at modesty will be for naught. This is how the Christian life works. To the extent that our behavior is not grounded in the grace of the gospel, our behavior is not authentically Christian and so cannot bear the fruits of authentic Christianity. Modesty is no exception. Pursue modesty outside of the gospel and not only will you fail to be genuinely modest, but everything you do in the name of that supposed modesty will undermine the very gospel you profess to believe.

- **If you are not convinced of the Father's love for you in Jesus, modesty will become for you a way of seeking to earn his acceptance.** *Maybe, just maybe, if I'm modest enough the heavenly Father will welcome me into his heart.*
- **If you are not convinced of the Father's love for you in Jesus, the call to modesty will feel like a chore.** It will seem as though the Lord is saddling you with a standard that sucks the joy right out of your life. Instead of seeing your mandate to be modest as a loving boundary erected by a Father who wants you to be happy, you'll see it as a restriction on happiness put in place by a cold and distant killjoy.
- **If you are not convinced of the Father's love for you in Jesus, you will see modesty as a way of getting a leg up on all the immodest people around you.** If you aren't resting in Jesus' righteousness, you'll just patch together your own counterfeit. You will grab for a comparative

righteousness—a standard you create or adapt from someone else, a standard that helps you feel like you are better than other people. And it will be nothing more than an effort to compensate for your feeling of insecurity before your heavenly Father.

The examples could go on, but the point here is simple: efforts at modesty without the gospel are actually anti-gospel because such efforts subtly but steadily communicate that God accepts us *on the basis of our performance*. This is why we can't overestimate the importance of letting the reality of the gospel increasingly grip our hearts.

As our understanding and practice of modesty is daily informed by the gospel, however, good things happen: we grow in godly discernment with respect to the standards of a particular culture, subculture, or situation, and this increasingly enables us to shine the light of the gospel clearly into whatever situation we may encounter.

No one did this better than Jesus.

The Comfort and the Call

There is a beautiful, true story in the gospel of John about a woman caught in the act of adultery. In John 7:53–8:11, Jewish leaders hope to trap Jesus with his words so they might legitimately charge him with heresy. They bring to him an adulteress who had apparently been caught in the act, saying, "The Law of Moses commanded us to stone such women. So what do you say?" Grace is so foreign to them— *gospel* is so far from their religious structures—that his answer blows their minds: "Let him who is without sin among you be the first to throw a stone at her."

Left speechless and feeling the sting of Jesus' words, the men leave the scene one by one until the only people left are Jesus and the woman. He asks her, "Woman, where are they? Has no one condemned you?" Of course, they've gone. He tells her that he doesn't condemn her either and sends her away to sin no more. Comfort, then a call to obedience. Grace with an edge.

The comfort: "Neither do I condemn you." What a wonderful statement about how free God's grace is! Even though this woman was guilty of a capital crime under the law of Moses, and even though we have no evidence that she was a disciple of Jesus, the Lord gave this merciful verdict: not condemned. And even though in ourselves we who actually *are* his disciples deserve nothing *but* condemnation, the gospel says, "There is therefore now no condemnation for those who are in Christ Jesus" (Romans 8:1).

So what should be our attitude toward people

who have offended against modesty? If Jesus Christ refused to condemn a woman caught in the very act of adultery, how should we relate to people who are caught in the act of immodesty?

It is far too easy for us to come down hard on people when they sin. But this is where we will go every time when we forget the gospel for ourselves—when we forget that each of us *is* the woman caught in the act who has nevertheless been exonerated by the blood and righteousness of Christ. Remembering the gospel will put us in the right frame of mind to behave toward the most immodest person—whether Christian or not—in a way that says, with absolute genuineness, "I do not condemn you." And when we find *ourselves* guilty of immodesty, remembering the gospel will likewise allow us to feel Jesus' acquittal.

The call: "Sin no more." Of course, "Neither do I condemn you" wasn't the only thing Jesus said to the woman. He said, "Neither do I condemn you; *go, and from now on sin no more*." This two-part response—neither condemning the woman nor commending her sin—is very instructive for us as believers.

First, it reminds us that, for the Christian, the Lord's acquittal comes *before* our pursuit of holiness. The removal of condemnation *precedes* the call to a godly life. You cannot go-and-sin-no-more your way into a relationship with God. The relationship itself is the ground and context for a life of obedience. Flip the order and you are not operating inside the gospel.

Second, Jesus' two-pronged response teaches us that he is serious about sin. Just because you are no longer under condemnation does not mean you have a free pass to keep on sinning. Whenever you find yourself thinking or behaving as if "no condemnation" amounts to divine permission to sin, look at the cross. Your acquittal cost the Father his beloved Son. He suffered, bled, died, and experienced the Father's wrath in order to *purchase* your acquittal. There was nothing free about it. This was a transaction with an unimaginable price. And Jesus didn't pay that price so that you would then be free to sin. He didn't do it to give you permission to indulge the flesh. He did it to give you the ability and the desire *not to* sin.

As the apostle Peter puts it, "You were ransomed from the futile ways inherited from your forefathers, not with perishable things such as silver or gold, but with the precious blood of Christ, like that of a lamb without blemish or spot" (1 Peter 1:18–19). If it cost something as precious as Jesus' blood to ransom you from your sin, then sin must be very serious business indeed. Therefore, to blow off sin as inconsequential demonstrates that you live out of a muddied understanding of the gospel.

Application to Immodesty in the Church

How do we bring the "sin no more" component of this story to bear in our interactions with others? How closely should we follow Jesus' example in this story? Fairly closely, but with wisdom. We need not explicitly incorporate both the *comfort* and the *call* in our response to others every time we encounter immodesty. Certainly, both elements should *inform* our *overall* response, but in any given situation, there are many factors that can and should legitimately influence both the content and manner of our response. We should be careful not to press this account beyond its intended purpose.

Think about your relationships with non-Christians. There may be times to raise the issue of sinful behavior when talking to unbelievers about modesty, but we should be quick to remember that we are not the Savior sent from heaven. So let's not go around telling immodestly dressed non-Christians to "leave our presence and sin no more." That probably wouldn't go over too well.

But what about when we encounter immodesty among Christians—whether ourselves or others? Then, we should emulate Jesus' two-pronged response to the woman caught in adultery quite closely. In those moments when we have opportunity to bring the truth of the gospel to bear on something as concrete and commonplace as immodesty, we must bring—to ourselves first, and only then to anyone else—both the *comfort* and the *call* of the gospel.

- The comfort: on the one hand, we express clearly and warmly that there is no sin that a Christian can commit that will relegate him or her to a place outside of God's family. This affirms their standing as our brother or sister in Christ.
- The call: on the other hand, we also express clearly and warmly that immodesty has no place in the life of a Christian. This admonishes them as our brother or sister in Christ for their sin of immodesty.

The gospel and modesty ought to intersect in this very tangible, honest, loving, and helpful way precisely at the point where people have been "caught in the act."

Being a Good Student of Culture

Let's return to the tricky question of how Christians can and should bring the gospel to bear when non-Christians are displaying immodesty. In chapter two, we defined modesty like this: *Modesty is that virtue which is respectful of a culture's rules for appropriate and inappropriate dress, speech, and behavior in a given situation.*

Really? Is it truly necessary—or, you may want to ask, is it truly *right*—for us as Christians to allow varying cultural and subcultural standards to influence what is seen as acceptable dress? Our answer would be, "As a general rule, yes, it is both right and necessary." In fact, we believe it is only the application of the gospel to valid cultural norms regarding dress that will allow your judgment of what is and is not modest in a given circumstance to be legitimately Christian.

Tim Keller explains how the gospel rightly shapes our approach to matters of culture, including standards of modesty:

> The liberal approach is to relativize all cultures. ("We can all get along because there is no truth.") The conservatives believe there is truth for evaluation of cultures, and so they choose some culture as superior and then they idolize it, feeling superior to others in the impulse of self-justifying pride.

> The gospel leads us to be: a) on the one hand, somewhat critical of all cultures, including our own (since there is truth), but b) on the other hand, we are morally superior to no one. After

all, we are saved by grace alone. Christians will exhibit both moral conviction yet compassion and flexibility.[6]

In other words, the gospel is the only thing that can lead us to see culture in a truly even-handed way. If we fail to hold firmly to the gospel, our tendency will be to a mix of demonization and idolization.

Demonization. Christians living in the West have consistently leaned toward demonizing secular culture, lamenting what Robert H. Bork called a culture-wide "slouching towards Gomorrah" (his 1996 bestselling book carried that title). From this stance, the trumpets blast to "take back America" and reclaim our original moral moorings. Because of this, Christians have a tendency not only to blame secular culture for the problem of immodesty in the church but also to adopt a siege mentality when it comes to culture generally — to build a wall to protect ourselves from it.

Idolization. The other side of that same coin is idolization, which is typically a mix of prideful motives and somewhat arbitrary choices. We raise a standard of modesty (again, often communicated through lists, measurements, diagrams, and the like) that 1) doesn't apply well across a range of cultures and subcultures, and 2) is rarely much more than the elevation of whatever practice and pattern seems most familiar and comfortable to a particular Christian or group of Christians.

The twin approaches of demonization and idolization have their roots in legalism. But there is also a third approach Christians can take when weighing secular culture: divinization is an unhelpful and counterproductive approach that has roots firmly planted in the soil of antinomianism.

Divinization. Some Christians in North America—following the lead of a number of well-known preachers from Generation X and younger—seem to have set aside the very concept of decency. A recent example is a book on marriage written by Mark Driscoll, pastor of the Seattle megachurch Mars Hill, and his wife. The book takes a more-or-less uncensored approach to discussing the marriage bed. Indeed, parts of it would make the buns on the heads of the little old ladies in your church come unraveled.

Some have said the book is a helpful corrective, but we see it as an example of the error we are calling divinization. This is a process by which cultural norms—norms that are themselves at odds with the tenor and teaching of Scripture—are implicitly granted a level of authority that competes with Scripture. We see this in the fact that those who approve of the book's racier sections take the view that the church's refusal to discuss sexual intimacy directly has left Christians — who are, after all, living in a culture run amok with titillating sexuality — with no clear, honest instruction or guidance on sexuality from a biblical standpoint. The controlling factor, from their perspective, is the intensity and pervasiveness of sexuality in the culture. In order to reach people with a helpful message about sexuality, proponents of this perspective feel that Christian writers must take their cues from the cultural approach to sexuality, even perhaps to a degree that violates the biblical standards of decency, propriety, lewdness, and respect for sexual intimacy. In effect, cultural norms are so intense that some feel compelled to give them greater credence than the Word of God.

Our purpose here is not to critique any particular book or sermon in detail but to highlight this general perspective that we believe exalts the culture over Scripture; it makes culture divine and God-like, and drops the Bible down a notch as our guide to what is appropriate.

Divinization results from too much "comfort" and not enough "call." It represents a failure of discernment. It accepts and approves a relaxation of biblical standards, or even a total re-assessment of those standards, in the hope of finding common ground with unbelievers.

Why do some Christians take this approach to modesty? Because they follow the lead of the surrounding culture, and they do that because they feel they must in order to reach people. We have no reason to doubt that their motivations are good, but the gospel should cause us to be simultaneously world-affirming and world-critical. We should say, as the theologians of old put it, *sic et non* (yes *and* no) about everything. That is, we should affirm what is good in our culture while also critiquing what is not good. We should realize that the line between good and evil isn't etched between aspects of our culture, but within things. Within everything, in fact, because everything about this world is fallen.

In order to say *sic et non* about everything, we must analyze our culture faithfully. We must observe it carefully with a view to respecting its rules for appropriate and inappropriate dress, speech, and behavior in given situations, but we must do this without walling it all out or welcoming it all in. The only way we can do this is if we have a robust faith in the gospel of grace. This puts us in "the gospel position"—the position from which we can live sensibly, respectfully, and lovingly within our culture's rules for modesty but also object conscientiously to immodesty when we see it.

So we see that the gospel and modesty intersect at the level of the heart—our heart's posture toward our culture. We must take a charitable posture toward our culture if we will ever hope to approach modesty from a Christian perspective.

No Simple Task

It should be fairly clear by now that to approach modesty from the vantage point of the gospel is not at all an easy thing. It's hard work—the hard work of faith in Christ and self-examination and loving our neighbor. We know that you'd rather it be a whole lot easier. "Bring out the charts and graphs!" or "Give me a list!" you say. And the reason we know that you'd like a Christian approach to modesty to be a whole lot easier is that we would, too!

Yet when all is said and done, no Christian really wants a list because we all know that if we could have been saved by a list of rules, Christ never would have come, and we would still be in our sins. No, gospel modesty is worth it no matter how hard it is. Every Christian wants to live on the corner of Modesty Avenue and Gospel Street, where grace and virtue intersect.

Five
WHY WE'RE NOT MODEST

Why is it so hard to implement the definition of modesty we are working with in this book? Why can't we more easily be considerate of other people and of the cultural and situational norms that call us to dress, speak, and behave appropriately in a given context? Yes, in many situations it can be tricky to discern the controlling norms, but the challenge is bigger even than that. Even when we rightly discern and genuinely understand those norms, there is another reason we so often behave immodestly.

It's because we're idolaters.

When we step over the modesty line, which we do regularly, we do so because of a whole range of idolatrous desires lurking just below the surface. These idols—Christ-substitutes and Christ-counterfeits—lure us away from modesty. Indeed, we express our devotion to false gods through immodesty of every kind. If we are to learn to be truly modest, we must get a handle on the ever-present temptations and realities of idolatry, for it is in the wildly varied pull and appeal of idolatry that the roots of all our immodesty lie.

It may seem strange to think that underneath our immodesty is idolatry. After all, a Christian is someone who has "turned *to* God *from* idols to serve the living and true God" (1 Thessalonians 1:9). But we're still sinners, which means that idolatry is always a threat. We think we are sophisticated and modern and far beyond idolatry, but we are fooling ourselves. We are all idolaters at heart, even if our idols are a little more up-to-date than carved wood or stone.

Idolatry is Universal

Consider the record of idolatry found in Scripture. A brief survey of the Old Testament reveals idolatry as *the central issue* for the Israelites.

Patriarchy. Joshua 24:2 summed up the situation in patriarchal times: "From ancient times your fathers lived beyond the River, namely, Terah, the father of Abraham and the father of Nahor, and they *served other gods.*"

Captivity and Exodus. Fast forward through the centuries and Ezekiel tells us that the sons of Israel practiced idolatry while in Egyptian captivity. Then, even after seeing all that the Lord had done to thwart and expose Egypt's false gods, they quickly regressed into their idolatrous practices following the exodus. With Aaron's help, they produced a golden calf and ascribed their deliverance to it. It's hard to miss the implied combination of Egyptian and Israeli religion, complete with its sacred animals, the general idea being something like, "Behold, Yahweh the calf!"

Judges. The time of the judges saw an unrelenting swing back and forth between faithfulness to the Lord and idolatry. Consider Judges 10:6 as a representative example:

> Then the sons of Israel again did what was evil in the sight of the LORD and served the Baals and the Ashtaroth, the gods of Syria, the gods of Sidon, the gods of Moab, the gods of the Ammonites, and the gods of the Philistines. And they forsook the LORD and did not serve him.

Monarchy. Every phase of the monarchy—early, middle, and late—was strewn with the refuse of idolatry.

- Solomon provided places of worship for all his foreign wives and all their foreign gods (see 1 Kings 11:7–8).
- Ahab provoked God more than any king before him had (see 1 Kings 16:30–33).

- Manasseh topped them all by building altars for foreign gods in the Temple, sacrificing his own son, and practicing witchcraft (see 1 Kings 21:1–6).

Exile. Idolatry then remained prevalent in Israel prior to and following the fall of Jerusalem. Just read the book of Ezekiel and you will see that Israel is indicted repeatedly for its idolatry during this period.

New Testament. Sad to say, we cannot look on idolatry in the Old Testament as any kind of special case. The fact that the New Testament offers so many commands regarding idolatry indicates it was still a significant issue. Consider these passages from the apostle Paul's first letter to the Corinthians:

- "I am writing to you not to associate with anyone who bears the name of brother if he is . . . an idolater . . . not even to eat with such a one" (5:11).
- "Or do you not know that the unrighteous will not inherit the kingdom of God? Do not be deceived: . . . idolaters . . . will [not] inherit the kingdom of God" (6:9–10).
- "Do not be idolaters as some of [the Israelites] were" (10:7a).
- "Therefore, my beloved, flee from idolatry" (10:14).

Paul address other churches with this same language of idolatry. He warns the churches of Galatia that those who practice idolatry will not inherit the kingdom of God (Galatians 5:20-21). He also commands the saints at Colossae to consider the members of their earthly bodies as dead to immorality, impurity, passion, evil desire, and greed, which *amount to idolatry* (Colossians 3:5). And the apostle John concludes his letter with the warning: "Little children, keep yourselves from idols" (1 John 5:21).

Us. I'm guessing you have probably never—not even once—cut down a tree, carved into it a crude image of an animal, inlayed the image with precious metals, set up the image on a pillar, and offered sacrifices to it. Not a likely scenario for anyone who might come across this book. Therefore, you may be thinking that while the cultures of the Ancient Near East and the Greco-Roman world of the first century were idolatrous, such behavior does not happen today—at least not among you and your peers.

But consider again all the statue and totem stuff that so dominates the Old Testament and has its echoes in the New Testament: while those actions represent culturally influenced *expressions* of idolatry, they are not the idolatry *itself*. In essence, idolatry has exactly *nothing* to do with statues and everything to do with your heart. Paul was making the same point when he said that heart sins *amount to idolatry*.

So don't be distracted by the imagery of crude statues and pagan sacrifices: the Bible everywhere conceives of idolatry as an issue of the heart. The physical manufacture of gods of our own design is merely a symptom of the disease of an idolatrous heart. Ezekiel got firsthand instruction about this from the Lord:

> Son of man, these men *have taken their idols into their hearts* and have set the stumbling block of their iniquity before their faces. Should I indeed let myself be consulted by them? Therefore speak to them and say to them, Thus says the Lord GOD: Any one of the house of Israel who *takes his idols into his heart* and sets the stumbling block of his iniquity before his face, and yet comes to the prophet, I the LORD will answer him as he comes with the multitude of his idols, that I may lay hold of *the hearts of the house of Israel, who are all estranged from me through their idols.* (14:3–5)

The elders of Israel "set up their idols in their hearts." This is where all idolatry begins. Our idols are idols of the *heart* long before they become something external. There is just as much idolatry today among the people of God as there ever was in the Old Testament. The external manifestations just look different. As with all sin, idolatrous estrangement from God begins in the heart.

Reflecting on Israel's idolatry, the great Genevan reformer John Calvin wrote, "From this fact let us learn how greatly our nature inclines us toward idolatry, rather than, by charging the Jews with being guilty of the common failing, we, under vain enticements to sin, sleep the sleep of death."[7] And again: "From this we may gather that man's nature, so to speak, is a perpetual factory of idols."[8]

Idolatry is part of our make-up. In our sin, it is who we are. Our nature perpetually manufactures idols. The history of humanity since the fall into sin is a history of idolatry.

Idolatry Is Adultery

The fact that idolatry begins in the heart explains why the most common image for idolatry in the Bible is not a statue at all. It's the image of adultery. And like all adultery, idolatry is something that takes place in violation of a marriage vow.

The Old Testament picture begins with Yahweh's relationship to Israel portrayed as the covenant bond of marriage:

> For your Maker is your husband,
>   the LORD of hosts is his name;
> and the Holy One of Israel is your Redeemer,

the God of the whole earth he is called.
For the LORD has called you,
like a wife deserted and grieved in spirit,
like a wife of youth when she is cast off. (Isaiah
54:5–6)

Whenever the people of God engage in idolatry—
whenever they forsake the Lord their God for
idols—they are described as an unfaithful bride,
an adulteress. Listen to God speak to the prophet
Jeremiah: "Surely, as a treacherous wife leaves her
husband, so have you been treacherous to me, O
house of Israel" (Jeremiah 3:20).

No single writer of Scripture expresses this more
vividly than Hosea. You'll remember that the Lord
asks Hosea to take for himself a wife of harlotry in
order that Israel, through Hosea, might know the
true nature of "her" (Israel's) unfaithfulness. The
Lord tells Hosea to "Go again, love a woman who is
loved by another man and is an adulteress, even as the
LORD loves the children of Israel, though they turn to
other gods and love cakes of raisins" (Hosea 3:1).

If the notion of adultery does not drive home
that idolatry is a heart issue, nothing else will. And
if we are willing to unpack the image of adultery a
bit further, we will find that it gives us even greater
insight into the nature of our own idolatry.

Think about it. What happens in an adulterous

relationship? What happens, for instance, when a wife cheats on her husband? She breaks her love compact with her spouse by setting her love upon another man—a man who is not her husband. There is a transfer of her affection from the one she promised to love to one whom she has "forsaken" and therefore promised never to love. It is not that she has become bereft of feelings of passion or affection; it is simply that she has transferred them to someone else.

It is the same with spiritual adultery. When we set our desire and passion and affection on something or someone other than God, we actually commit adultery against him. And all of us are capable—we know this too well—of transferring our affection from God to someone or something else. Almost anything else!

Whatever draws our worship away from the one true and living God qualifies as an idol. Metaphorically speaking, we still manufacture and offer sacrifices to all sorts of things other than God. In light of this truth and from the perspective of those who are guilty, we ought to see our idolatry from four perspectives:

- Idolatry is vain
- Idolatry is violent
- Idolatry is vile
- Idolatry is vindictive

The Vanity of Idolatry

The Lord repeatedly tries to persuade us of the vanity of our idolatry. Our idols make all kinds of promises that they cannot deliver on—not for a second. The prophet Jeremiah says they are like broken cisterns that can hold no water and like a scarecrow in a cucumber field. They are false advertising, guaranteed futility, bridges to nowhere. Isaiah may make the vanity of our idolatry clearer than any other prophet does:

> All who fashion idols are nothing, and the things they delight in do not profit. Their witnesses neither see nor know, that they may be put to shame. . . .

> The ironsmith takes a cutting tool and works it over the coals. He fashions it with hammers and works it with his strong arm. He becomes hungry, and his strength fails; he drinks no water and is faint. The carpenter stretches a line; he marks it out with a pencil. He shapes it with planes and marks it with a compass. He shapes it into the figure of a man, with the beauty of man, to dwell in a house. He cuts down cedars, or he chooses a cypress tree or an oak and lets it grow strong among the trees of the forest. He plants a cedar and the rain nourishes it. Then it becomes

fuel for a man. He takes a part of it and warms himself; he kindles a fire and bakes bread. Also, he makes a god and worships it; he makes it an idol and falls down before it. Half of it he burns in the fire. Over the half he eats meat; he roasts it and is satisfied. Also he warms himself and says, "Aha, I am warm, I have seen the fire!" And the rest of it he makes into a god, his idol, and falls down to it and worships it. He prays to it and says, "Deliver me, for you are my god!" . . .

No one considers, nor is there knowledge or discernment to say, "Half of it I burned in the fire; I also baked bread on its coals; I roasted meat and have eaten. And shall I make the rest of it into an abomination? Shall I fall down before a block of wood?" He feeds on ashes; a deluded heart has led him astray, and he cannot deliver himself or say, "Is there not a lie in my right hand?" (Isaiah 44:9, 12–17, 19–20)

In addition to showing us very vividly the folly of idolatry, Isaiah 44 gives us even greater insight into what's going on in our hearts when we commit idolatry. The last verse above says, "A deluded heart has led him astray." That is, the idolatrous heart believes a lie that idols can actually *do* something—that they can deliver what we want from them. But they cannot do that. They are lifeless creations of our own imaginations.

How vain is our pursuit of our idols! They are utterly impotent. *They* need *us* for their existence. And the only power they have is the power we give them by setting our affections on them and believing the ridiculous notion that they are superior to the Lord or can give us something good that the Lord cannot or will not give us. The idols of our hearts will never bring us lasting satisfaction, true joy, or real victory. We need to stop believing the lie that something or someone other than Jesus Christ can make us truly happy. This is really what we're saying in all our idolatry: "I need _____ plus Jesus to make me happy. Jesus is not enough."

This is why the apostle James says in the fourth chapter of his letter that the source of our quarrels and conflicts is our adulterous/idolatrous hearts— our desires "wage war" in our members. That war is between Jesus Christ and all our would-be saviors— between Jesus and everything else that we would desire over him.

So if you want some insight into the nature of your own idolatry, you need to ask yourself what you desire in addition to or apart from Jesus in order to be truly happy. What do you crave? For what are you willing to sin? And what do you throw a sin tantrum about when you don't get it?

You may realize that you made an immodest dress choice, but when you press the "why" question, you realize that the reason you made that choice was that you wanted approval from others. You may realize you bragged about an occupational achievement, or were rude at a dinner party, but when you press the why question you realize you want to be seen as special or smarter or superior in some way. In that moment what others thought was more important to you than what God thought, and you were willing to sin against modesty to get their attention. This calls for repentance, not just of the immodesty but of the heart issue that produced it.

Think of it like this: your immodesty is the fruit on a tree with an idolatrous root. Your sin against modesty shows you that at heart level you are living for something or someone other than Jesus Christ. And the sad thing is that even when we get the thing we crave, the idol can't deliver on it. It can't give us the satisfaction we were made for. More than that, even when it does deliver some counterfeit version of the satisfaction of Christ, it immediately pounces. This is the violence of idolatry.

The Violence of Idolatry

Psalms 115:8 and 135:18 say that those who make idols will become like them. This means that we become dehumanized by our idolatrous desires, much like Smeagol from *The Lord of the Rings* was reduced to the creature Gollum because of his 500-year devotion to his "precious," the evil ring of power. When something or someone becomes more precious to you than Jesus Christ, you begin to become less than human. The idol gradually destroys you.

Pastor Dick Kaufmann of Harbor Presbyterian Church in San Diego, California, talks about the violence of idolatry in terms of "raising the bar" and "lowering the boom." When the idol makes good on what it promises—that affirmation, that double-take, that approval—it immediately raises the bar, saying, "That's not enough. You need more." Thus, even when you get what you want, what you want is never enough. Eventually, this turns into a deep sense of disillusionment: "Is this all there is? What's the point?"

On the flip side, when you don't get the thing your idol promises, your idol lowers the boom by making you feel guilty and foolish and ashamed and anxious: "What's wrong with me? I can't believe I did that. What an idiot I am! What do I need to do to make it work this time?" From here, if you continue to fail, your life becomes miserable, moving from one colossal failure to the next.

Use this as an incentive to avoid immodesty. Not just the outward manifestation, but the sin at the root of your immodesty. Say to yourself something like this:

I only want to dress or speak or behave immodestly in this situation because I believe that it will get me something—something promised to me by a false god. But a false god can only promise a false good. This idol does not want to bless me—it wants to hurt me and own me and keep me as its slave. Don't believe the lie. Don't give in.

The Vileness of Idolatry

Our idolatry is not only *vain*, in that it fails to bring us true and lasting satisfaction. It is not only *violent*, in that it seeks to enslave us. It is also *vile*, in that it utterly offends the Lord.

In the Bible, idolatry is consistently called an *abomination* to the Lord. It is totally and completely revolting to him, a form of rebellion against him whereby we refuse to be thankful for who he is and all that he has done for us. Romans 1 couldn't be clearer:

> For the wrath of God is revealed from heaven against all ungodliness and unrighteousness of men, who by their unrighteousness suppress the truth. For what can be known about God is plain to them, because God has shown it to them. For his invisible attributes, namely, his eternal power

and divine nature, have been clearly perceived, ever since the creation of the world, in the things that have been made. So they are without excuse. For although they knew God, they did not honor him as God or give thanks to him, but they became futile in their thinking, and their foolish hearts were darkened. Claiming to be wise, they became fools, and exchanged the glory of the immortal God for images resembling mortal man and birds and animals and creeping things.

Therefore God gave them up in the lusts of their hearts to impurity, to the dishonoring of their bodies among themselves, because they exchanged the truth about God for a lie and worshiped and served the creature rather than the Creator, who is blessed forever! Amen. (Romans 1:18–25)

The reason God gave us over to our sin is explicit: we became idolatrous. God thinks our idolatry is vile. Every idolatrous thought, act, and behavior undermines the magnification of his glory.

But more than finding it vile for the offense it gives him, the Lord finds it vile because of what it does to his people. Amazingly, Judges 10:16 says that Israel got rid of the foreign gods among them and served the Lord, and then that the Lord got impatient with the misery Israel felt afterwards. Smashing their idols made them miserable, but God couldn't bear it. He hated to see them so miserable.

God knows that your idolatry makes you miserable and he hates to see you that way. Idolatry isn't only vile to God because of what it does to him but because of what it does to you! This leads us to the fourth characteristic of idolatry: the vindictiveness of idolatry.

The Vindictiveness of Idolatry

When you realize how the Lord's heart breaks for you in your idolatry (both *for* you and *because of* you) and when you realize just how much he loves you in Jesus, you begin to see your idolatry as something cruel and vindictive on your part. Why would you want to sin against such love? Why would you live for and long for anything or anyone other than the Lord?

For Christians, this is a huge disincentive to idolatry: we don't want to break God's heart. It kills us to read Ezekiel 6:9:

> Then those of you who escape will remember me among the nations where they are carried captive, how I have been broken over their whoring heart that has departed from me and over their

eyes that go whoring after their idols. And they will be loathsome in their own sight for the evils which they have committed, for all their abominations.

Idolators will regret their idolatry—it will be loathsome to them. Idolatry is vain, violent, vile, and vindictive. And it underlies all our immodest behavior.

This is why we're not modest: we have a worship problem. We worship at altars that lead us to sin against modesty. Don't see your immodesty as the *root* of the problem; see it as the *fruit* and go after the plant where you can do the most damage—the tangled roots of your idolatrous desires.

Six
WHERE TO GO FROM HERE

Despite everything we've said in this book—even after all the language about how modesty can't be captured in a set of rules—be honest with yourself. At some level, don't you expect us now to give you a set of rules? Or at least a list or some really concrete, specific guidelines?

At some level, don't you wish we *could*?

It would feel so good just to have two simple lists. You could take one to your closet, possibly with a big garbage bag in hand. You could tuck the other into your wallet or your purse, or store it in your phone—to review before your next small group meeting or dinner party or office event so that you don't say or do something immodest.

For our own sakes and for the gospel's, we will not go there. To give you any kind of list would simply replace immodesty with legalism; you might feel better for a while, but we'd all be missing the heart of the issue. Instead, we'll start our final chapter with a reminder of three key points:

Modesty is largely a question of situational and cultural context. Again, this means that the culture and situation substantially (although not exclusively) determine what is appropriate and inappropriate.

Yes, there are some biblical lines we ought never to cross. But under the authority of Scripture, good students of the gospel are sensitive to each situation and culture, and they respond appropriately. They desire to be both biblically and contextually modest for one reason: so that they can honor God and be good representatives of the gospel without needlessly erecting barriers to communication.

The modesty spectrum has two poles. In any given situation or culture, the bounds of modesty can be violated in a conservative direction or a liberal direction. Speech, behavior, and dress can be too wild or too mild. Gospel wisdom is present to help us with either extreme.

If we understand the gospel, we will be hesitant to ascribe corrupt or sinful motives to edgier kinds of speech, behavior, or dress. By the same token, when faced with more conservative speech, behavior, or dress, we will be hesitant to ascribe prudish or puritanical motives.[9] We will consistently recognize that, while all we can really ever see is the outward behavior, God sees the heart, and perfectly so.

Actual immodesty isn't always a sin. This one can drive some well-intentioned Christians kind of crazy, but it's true.

Let's assume someone has acted, spoken, or dressed in a way that is *actually immodest based on the legitimate norms of a particular culture or subculture* (that is, norms that do not blatantly cross clear biblical lines). Two people may do that outwardly in almost exactly the same way, yet one of them is guilty of sin and the other is not. It depends on motivations and awareness. (And while both people would need correction, the kinds of correction should differ considerably.)

Sinful immodesty is always a question of the heart. For example, if you come to know that a brother or sister in Christ is dressing immodestly for the sake of arousing lust in the opposite sex, his or her immodesty has moved from the arena of immodesty to the arena of immorality. Or if you come to know that a person is using questionable language for the sake of "getting the prudes to relax," his or her immodesty has moved from the arena of immodesty to the arena of lovelessness.

With these reminders in place, we will offer several suggestions to move you toward a modest life.

Pressing Toward Modesty

Dig up the roots. Start with yourself. You may already have some handle on your own immodesty, but take the next step: ask a trusted friend whether he or she sees you as a modest person, making sure you use a gospel-centered understanding of that word. Then review chapter five and go for the idolatrous root of your own immodest speech, behavior, or dress.

If all you do is hold your tongue or change your wardrobe or moderate your behavior without doing the hard work of unearthing the idolatrous desires that led to your immodesty in that area, you will not be much different from a modest non-Christian. Remember that behavior is incidental to the heart; behavior is the indicator that the Lord uses to help you discover the structures of worship that lie beneath your behavior. You could dress in Amish garb, even determining that buttons are too flashy, and still be entirely immodest at heart. You could determine never to raise your voice or draw attention to yourself in any way and do it all out of pride rather than modesty. Altering behavior is not enough because altering behavior is not the point.

Pay close attention. Be sensitive to whatever situation you find yourself in. It is very easy to approach unfamiliar social and cultural situations like a bull in a china shop instead of like a mature believer. Ask yourself and others what the given situation requires. Is there anything that would be considered rude or unseemly? If there is, avoid it and move instead toward behavior appropriate to the context. Be sure that you are paying more attention to what the Bible says about dress and demeanor than what culture says; the Bible is the only sure and unfailing guide we have. The culture around us will be wrong more often than it is right.

Think twice. Consider the potential effect of your behaviors or dress on others. A woman may not in reality be sinning against modesty by choosing a certain dress, but that doesn't mean that the choice is a loving act to her brothers in Christ. It may be that your culturally and situationally appropriate outfit causes men to stumble. It may be that your "freedom" to use language that others find troubling violates their consciences. What's the point of that? The grace of God makes us willing to give up our rights for the sake of weaker members of the body of Christ. Knowing how much grace you received, and at what cost, makes you willing to extend that grace to other people.

Restrain the rush to judgment. Refuse to make a person's modesty a litmus test of his or her orthodoxy. If you think—or worse, if you *say*—that such-and-such a man must not be a Christian because he's given to boasting, or that such-and-such a woman must not be a Christian because of the length of her skirt, you are forgetting the reality of the persistent problem of indwelling sin and the great variance in spiritual maturity among Christians.

Sin and immaturity are not "if" questions in the

Christian life; they are "when" questions. The issue is what the Christian does with his or her sin and immaturity. If someone is quick to repent, seek forgiveness, and move toward reconciliation and greater maturity, he or she is manifesting godly character. For any of us to turn immodesty into a salvation issue is to fall into a far worse sin: hypocrisy.

Preach it! A better or more universal piece of counsel has rarely been given: preach the gospel to yourself every day. Keep the gospel front-and-center in your life—this is the only way you will avoid seeing adherence to cultural conventions as an oppressive straightjacket on the one hand or as a ground for acceptance with God on the other. As we said earlier, when the gospel controls your modesty, everything changes.

When the gospel controls your modesty, you want to be modest because God sent his son, Jesus, to *die* for your immodesty, and especially because Jesus *willingly* died for it.

When the gospel controls your modesty, you no longer see it as a way of putting God in your debt, because you don't need to twist God's arm to accept you—he already accepts you freely and fully in Jesus Christ!

APPENDIX

Of Modesty and Men

Most of the time, immodesty is framed with respect to how it appears in women. Therefore, it may be helpful to try to point out some ways in which men can be immodest. One good way to do that is to offer concrete examples.

Now, throughout this book we have made a big deal about how there is no list you can follow in order to remain modest. We really believe that's true — that lists in this area can only lead to legalism. But the irony is that the kind of concrete examples we are about to offer can look like a list labeled "Don't Do This"! Please understand that this is not our intention. In this appendix we want to equip you to recognize immodesty in men by giving you examples, but we certainly don't mean for the examples to become a list in themselves. We hope you will keep that in mind as you read.

* * *

A few years ago Tim attended a wedding where one couple stood out from the rest. She was wearing a way-too-tight, way-too-low, way-too-short, way-too-everything dress that at one time or another drew the eye of every man there; if the dress didn't do it, the stilettos certainly did. But that wasn't even the most memorable part. On her arm was a man wearing a shining white suit that must have cost more than the wedding itself, shoes that could have funded the honeymoon and, just for good measure, a remarkable hat and cane.

Neither the man nor the woman seemed at all respectful of their context, of the culture around them, or of their hosts. Their attire and manner did not serve the other guests or the bride and groom. Wherever they went, eyes and conversation followed them. This appeared to be exactly what they had intended.

By any definition, both of them were being immodest, but each in a different way. It seemed like she was out to draw the eye of the men around her, and thus to have power over them (which she did!). But it seemed that his intention was to display his wealth, demonstrate his sense of style, and declare his superiority.

This may be an unusually stark example, but it shouldn't surprise anyone that men can be immodest, too. We are subject to the same temptations toward vanity and self-glorification that women are. It's just that we tend to express our immodesty differently.

So here we want take an opportunity to speak directly to men, encouraging you to consider that you too may have your own struggles with modesty. As we begin, let's remind ourselves of the definition of modesty—*that virtue that is respectful of a culture's rules for appropriate and inappropriate dress, speech, and behavior in a given situation or a given context*. Because this definition is genderless it assumes, rightly, that a man can be immodest in his dress, his speech, or any other area of life. Yes, even guys can be immodest.

Modest Attire

Look at my physique. Women are not alone in wanting to be seen and noticed and recognized for their physical attributes. A man who admires his own physique can likewise be tempted to dress in a way that immodestly displays his body. His motivations may differ somewhat from those of the immodestly dressed woman, but the idolatry at the root of his clothing choices are essentially the same. It is wise to be fit, and there is nothing wrong with a toned physique, but dressing to impress others with your physical attributes serves yourself at the expense of others.

Check out my clothes. A man need not draw

attention to his body to be dressed immodestly. He may instead aim to draw attention to his clothing and the claims or statements that clothing makes.

One man may want to make a point about his wealth or position or status (actual or supposed), so he puts on an Armani suit to attend an inner-city church, trying to prove how much more he owns than everyone else. He wears only the best brands and makes sure that everything fits just so. He consistently overdresses on purpose. Instead of being known for his godliness, he becomes known, he hopes, as a man of high style or good taste.

Another man may use his clothing to make a statement about culture. This can take all kinds of forms, either dressing up or dressing down regardless of what seems appropriate to the situation. One man might wear a suit to church every Sunday even when everyone else dresses casually — not because he is convicted in his conscience that he ought to do this, and not even because he is showing off, but because he wants to show the young people around him how they "ought to dress." His wardrobe is an outgrowth of a judgmental heart. Another man might wear jeans and a T-shirt to church when everyone else dresses far more formally — he wants to show them that they should loosen up, that they need to get over their old-fashioned social mores.

Each of these are examples of immodesty

because the motivations underlying them are self-focused and self-glorifying. These motivations produce actions that are disrespectful and unloving and ultimately call attention to self instead of to the Lord. The Christian should be eager to be over-looked, eager to go unseen or forgotten, if that is what will best glorify the Lord. God wants us to be known for godly character, which cannot be worked out in a gym and has no connection to wealth. The man known for his extravagant or form-fitting clothing is a man known for things that matter little in God's economy.

No, men are not at all immune to the tempta-tion to dress immodestly. Like women, we can be tempted to wear clothing that is an expression of our idolatrous hearts, hearts that want to be known for all the wrong things.

Modest Speech

We live at a time when practically no topic of conver-sation is off-limits, where words and ideas that were recently considered shameful (or at least private) are mentioned boldly from the television screen and the news headlines. There is no sense of decorum—at least, none that overcomes our desire to be "authentic" and shocking. Many Christians proclaim that if everyone else is discussing such topics, and doing so without shame, we must meet them where they are.

But modesty is a virtue that allows us to control our speech. The implications of the gospel reach to the farthest extent of our character, touching our words, our topics of conversation, and even the ways in which we converse: "And whatever you do, in word or deed, do everything in the name of the Lord Jesus, giving thanks to God the Father through him" (Colossians 3:17). Modest speech is speech that draws attention to God rather than attention to ourselves; modest speech serves others and stays aware of the contexts in which we find ourselves.

The content of our conversation. The modest man understands that not every topic makes for appropriate conversation. His modesty compels him to avoid speaking of things that are vulgar or otherwise inappropriate: "Let no corrupting talk come out of your mouths, but only such as is good for building up, as fits the occasion, that it may give grace to those who hear" (Ephesians 4:29). Some topics corrupt instead of edify; they tear down instead of build up. A topic of conversation may be appropriate at certain times but not at other times; learn to discern what "fits the occasion." Modesty compels us to consider what is appropriate for any given situation, but immodesty draws us into discussing certain topics for their shock value, so that eyes and minds will be drawn to us, and we will be known for our bold, outside-the-box manner.

Paul even says that certain topics will *always* be inappropriate: "Let there be no filthiness nor foolish talk nor crude joking, which are out of place, but instead let there be thanksgiving" (Ephesians 5:4). A few verses later he says, "Take no part in the unfruitful works of darkness, but instead expose them. For it is shameful even to speak of the things that they do in secret" (Ephesians 5:11–12). Some things are so inappropriate and shameful that we should never discuss them at all.

The modest man is aware of the power of his words, so he chooses each one carefully, seeking to make each word an opportunity to bless and strengthen and build up. He is aware that one careless word can cause a great deal of damage, and he is willing to say very little if that is how he can bless others. Sometimes the most modest, helpful, and God-glorifying thing one can say is nothing at all.

The context of our conversation. Modesty compels us to be aware of the people to whom we are speaking. The preacher, especially one teaching on a sensitive topic, may be immodest in his speech if he does not suit his words to his audience. Rather than making sure that this words draw attention to the Lord, he may use words to draw attention to himself by being shocking or insensitive. Preaching on sexuality, for example, to an audience of men may be very different in content and vocabulary than preaching to an audience that includes women and children.

Both of the authors of this book are given opportunities to travel internationally to speak and preach. Both of us have learned the importance of studying the cultural context in order to restrain ourselves from deliberate or inadvertent immodesty. This allows us to better serve and better love the people we speak to. Preaching on sexuality may sound very different in Asia than it does in North America, for example, and this for the sake of modesty.

In every case, whether a preacher or not, the man concerned with modesty will do his best to understand his present context so that he can speak boldly but also humbly, not drawing attention away from Christ by violating written or unwritten rules of the culture.

The manner of our conversation. Have you ever been in a room where a person is having a private conversation at roof-raising volume? Do you know that person who always speaks far too loudly, who is far too boisterous, who has no self-awareness of how his voice is dominating the room? He may merely be ignorant of how loud his voice is and how he is drawing attention to himself, or he may be doing it because he wants people to notice him.

The man who talks loudly or laughs out loud when the atmosphere is subdued, perhaps at a somber occasion like a funeral, is probably a man demonstrating immodesty. Rather than altering his behavior to fit the occasion, he draws undue attention to himself and demonstrates disrespect to everyone around him.

We may be immodest when we speak about inappropriate topics, but we may also be immodest when we speak too loudly or too forcefully. This is a genuine temptation for the preacher or public speaker who wants to impress with his style. When we draw attention to the way we say things instead of to what we say, we step over the line into immodest speech. "Let your speech always be gracious, seasoned with salt" (Colossians 4:6).

Modest Behavior

Now, what is modest *behavior* for men? As with dress and speech, modest behavior avoids drawing inappropriate attention to self or to others. Rather, its goal is to edify—and again, what we should or should not do in order to edify others in a given context will depend a great deal on the context itself.

Let's be gentlemen, guys. Some customs long regarded as "gentlemanly" are nearly always consistent with modest behavior, like holding open a door or willingly and quickly giving up your seat to a woman or an elderly person. Courtesy is another gentlemanly expression of modesty, one that refuses to ignore others, whether actively (because you think too highly of yourself) or passively (because you are engrossed with your smart phone).

Your behavior influences others. Men should also pay careful attention to their behavior because of how it can encourage others toward either godliness or worldliness. Men can contribute to the immodesty (or modesty) of others—especially women—by *where they look* and *how they talk*. Women certainly bear their own responsibility for dressing modestly: they need to remember that God has designed men to be drawn to what is visually appealing and therefore it can actually be difficult for a man to look away instantly when he encounters an immodestly dressed woman. At the same time, no Christian man has an excuse for ogling the women around him: the fruit of the Holy Spirit, after all, includes self-control.

Indulge us with an illustration. We write as pastors who routinely make visits to hospitals in the hope of bringing comfort and encouragement to the people we love and serve. Yet there is very little modesty in a hospital. In fact, to be admitted to a hospital is to give up your modesty (and dignity!) and have it replaced with a too-short gown that has a permanent breeze in the back. This can pose challenges for those of us who walk the halls or stop in the rooms. Temptations to lust (and at times shock and revulsion) can appear around almost any corner. Every pastor needs to ensure that he can love the people he visits by keeping his eyes and his mind unaffected by what in any other context would be rank immodesty. A pastor who cannot exercise self-control in these circumstances is a pastor who will be unable to serve the people he visits.

There may be little hope for modesty in a hospital, but there is great hope for a growing culture of modesty in other contexts. You can do your part in creating a culture of modesty and honor for the women around you by guarding your heart and your eyes. When we regard women in the church first and foremost as sisters in Christ—not objects for us to gaze upon or lust after—we create a safe place for them to be the women God has made them to be. This is true regardless of the context and regardless of what they choose to wear. When we behave modestly outside of the church, we stand apart from others and live as lights in a dark world where all kinds of immodesty flourish. Modest behavior is a lifestyle of service, getting out of the way in order to point others to Jesus.

Gentlemen, we have served the church poorly by making modesty into an issue that only pertains to women. Let's take back modesty so that we too can serve God as men who take every opportunity to deny ourselves and serve others.

Endnotes

1. C. S. Lewis, *Mere Christianity* (San Francisco: Harper, 2002), 83–84.
2. See Matthew 15:19–20.
3. Lewis, *Mere Christianity*, 84.
4. J. I. Packer, *Knowing God* (Westmont, IL: InterVarsity, 1973), 120.
5. Tim Keller, "The Centrality of the Gospel," http://download. redeemer.com/pdf/learn/resources/Centrality_of_the_Gospel-Keller.pdf.
6. *Ibid.*
7. John Calvin, *Institutes of the Christian Religion*, trans. Ford Lewis Battles (Philadelphia: The Westminster Press, 1960), 1.11.3.
8. Calvin, *Institutes* 1.11.8.
9. See Lewis, *Mere Christianity*, 83–84.

About the Authors

R W Glenn is Pastor of Preaching and Vision at Redeemer Bible Church in Minnetonka, MN, and author of *Crucifying Morality: How the Teaching of Jesus Destroys Religion* (Shepherd Press, 2012). He blogs at solidfoodmedia.com.

Tim Challies is a pastor, blogger, author, and book reviewer. He has written *Sexual Detox: A Guide for Guys Who are Sick of Porn*; *The Discipline of Spiritual Discernment*; and *The Next Story*. Visit him at Challies.com and DiscerningReader.com.

The Organized Heart
A Woman's Guide to Conquering Chaos

by Staci Eastin

**Disorganized?
You don't need more rules, the
latest technique, or a new gadget.**

**This book will show you a different,
better way. A way grounded in the
grace of God.**

"Staci Eastin packs a gracious punch, full of insights about our
disorganized hearts and lives, immediately followed by the balm of
gospel-shaped hopes. This book is ideal for accountability partners
and small groups."

> ***Carolyn McCulley, blogger, filmmaker, author of* Radical Wom-
> anhood *and* Did I Kiss Marriage Goodbye?**

"Unless we understand the spiritual dimension of productivity, our
techniques will ultimately backfire. Find that dimension here. Encouraging and uplifting rather than guilt-driven, this book can help
women who want to be more organized but know that adding a new
method is not enough."

> ***Matt Perman, Director of Strategy at Desiring God, blogger,
> author of the forthcoming book,* What's Best Next: How the
> Gospel Transforms the Way You Get Things Done**

"Organizing a home can be an insurmountable challenge for a woman. The Organized Heart makes a unique connection between idols
of the heart and the ability to run a well-managed home. This is not
a how-to. Eastin looks at sin as the root problem of disorganization.
She offers a fresh new approach and one I recommend, especially to
those of us who have tried all the other self-help models and failed."

> ***Aileen Challies, mom of three, and wife of blogger, author, and
> pastor Tim Challies**

Who Am I?
Identity in Christ

by Jerry Bridges

Jerry Bridges unpacks Scripture to give the Christian eight clear, simple, interlocking answers to one of the most essential questions of life.

"Jerry Bridges' gift for simple but deep spiritual communication is fully displayed in this warm-hearted, biblical spelling out of the Christian's true identity in Christ."

> **J. I. Packer, *Theological Editor*, ESV Study Bible; *author*, Knowing God, A Quest for Godliness, Concise Theology**

"I know of no one better prepared than Jerry Bridges to write *Who Am I?* He is a man who knows who he is in Christ and he helps us to see succinctly and clearly who we are to be. Thank you for another gift to the Church of your wisdom and insight in this book."

> **R.C. Sproul, *founder, chairman, president, Ligonier Ministries; executive editor*, Tabletalk *magazine; general editor*, The Reformation Study Bible**

"*Who Am I?* answers one of the most pressing questions of our time in clear gospel categories straight from the Bible. This little book is a great resource to ground new believers and remind all of us of what God has made us through faith in Jesus. Thank the Lord for Jerry Bridges, who continues to provide the warm, clear, and biblically balanced teaching that has made him so beloved to this generation of Christians."

> **Richard D. Phillips, *Senior Minister, Second Presbyterian Church, Greenville, SC***

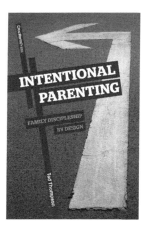

Intentional Parenting
Family Discipleship by Design
by Tad Thompson

The Big Picture and a Simple Plan — That's What You Need to Do Family Discipleship Well

This book will allow you to take all the sermons, teachings, and exhortations you have received on the topic of family discipleship, make sense of it, and put it to use.

"As parents, we know God has given us the responsibility to train our children in his ways. But many parents don't know where or how to start. Tad has done us all a favor by identifying seven key categories of biblical teaching we can utilize in teaching our children godly truth and principles. This easy-to-follow plan will help any parent put the truth of God's Word into their children's hearts."

> **Kevin Ezell, President, North American Mission Board, Southern Baptist Convention; father of six**

"Here is a practical page-turner that encourages fathers to engage the hearts of their families with truth and grace. In an age when truth is either ignored or despised, it is refreshing to see a book written for ordinary fathers who want their families to be sanctified by the truth. Thompson writes with a grace which reminds us that parenting flows from the sweet mercies of Christ."

> **Joel Beeke, President, Puritan Reformed Theological Seminary**

"Need an introductory text to the topic of discipling children? Here is a clear, simple book on family discipleship, centered on the gospel rather than human successes or external behaviors."

> **James M. Hamilton, Associate Professor of Biblical Theology, The Southern Baptist Theological Seminary**

Wrestling with an Angel

A Story of Love, Disability
and the Lessons of Grace

by Greg Lucas

**The riveting, inspiring true story
that readers have called
"a touchstone book of my life" and
"alternately hilarious and heart-
breaking," a book that
"turns the diamond of grace in
such a way that you see facets
you never really noticed before."**

"C.S. Lewis wrote that he paradoxically loved *The Lord of the Rings* because it 'broke his heart' – and Greg Lucas' writing does the same for me."
Justin Taylor, Managing Editor, ESV Study Bible

"Witty... stunning... striking... humorous and heartfelt. *Wrestling with an Angel* provides a fresh, honest look at one father's struggle to embrace God in the midst of his son's disability. Can sheer laughter and weeping gracefully coexist in a world of so much affliction? Greg knows all about it. I highly recommend this wonderfully personal book!"
Joni Eareckson Tada, Joni and Friends International

"You will laugh; you will cry. You will feel sick; you will feel inspired. You will be repulsed by the ugliness of sin; you will be overwhelmed by the love of God. Greg Lucas takes us on an unforgettable ride as he extracts the most beautiful insights into grace from the most painful experiences of life."
David P. Murray, Puritan Reformed Theological Seminary

"Greg Lucas is a captivating storyteller. When he writes about life with Jake, I recognize God's grace and loving persistence in my life. I want more!"
Noël Piper, author, and wife of pastor and author John Piper

Grieving, Hope and Solace
When a Loved One Dies in Christ

by Albert N. Martin

**There is comfort for the grief.
There are answers to the questions.
The Bible does offer hope, solace,
healing, and confidence.**

**Pastor Albert Martin has been
there.**

"This tender book by a much-loved pastor, written after the death of
his beloved wife, offers comfort to those in tears. A rare guidebook to
teach us how to grieve with godliness, it is relevant to us all – if not for
today, then no doubt for tomorrow."
Maurice Roberts, former editor, **Banner of Truth** *magazine*

"Albert N. Martin is a seasoned pastor, skilled teacher, and gifted writer
who has given us a priceless treasure in this book. All who read these
pages will, unquestionably, be pointed to Christ and find themselves
greatly helped."
Steve Lawson, Christ Fellowship Baptist Church, Mobile, AL

"Like turning the corner and being met by a glorious moonrise, or
discovering a painter or musician who touches us in the deepest
recesses of our being–this little book by Pastor Al Martin has been
such an experience for me. Whether you are a pastor or counselor,
one who is experiencing the pangs of grief, or a member of the
church who wants to be useful to others, you need to read this book."
Joseph Pipa, President, Greenville Presbyterian Theo. Sem.

"Personal tenderness and biblical teaching in a sweet book of comfort. Buy it and give it away, but make sure to get a copy for yourself."
Dr. Joel R. Beeke, President, Puritan Reformed Theo. Sem.

"But God..."

The Two Words at the Heart of the Gospel

by Casey Lute

Just two words.
Understand their use in Scripture,
and you will never be the same.

"Rock-solid theology packaged in an engaging and accessible form."
– *Louis Tullo, Sight Regained blog*

"Keying off of nine occurrences of "But God" in the English Bible, Casey Lute ably opens up Scripture in a manner that is instructive, edifying, encouraging, and convicting. This little book would be useful in family or personal reading, or as a gift to a friend. You will enjoy Casey's style, you will have a fresh view of some critical Scripture, and your appreciation for God's mighty grace will be deepened."
> *Dan Phillips, Pyromaniacs blog; author,* **The World-Tilting Gospel**

"A refreshingly concise, yet comprehensive biblical theology of grace that left this reader more in awe of the grace of God. "
> *Aaron Armstrong, BloggingTheologically. com*

"Casey Lute reminds us that nothing is impossible with God, that we must always reckon with God, and that God brings life out of death and joy out of sorrow."
> *Thomas R. Schreiner, Professor of New Testament Interpretation, The Southern Baptist Theological Seminary*

"A mini-theology that will speak to the needs of every reader of this small but powerful book. Read it yourself and you will be blessed. Give it to a friend and you will be a blessing."
> *William Varner, Prof. of Biblical Studies, The Master's College*

Smooth Stones
Bringing Down the Giant
Questions of Apologetics

by Joe Coffey

Street-level apologetics for everyday Christians.

Because faith in Jesus makes sense. And you don't need an advanced degree to understand why.

"What a thrill for me to see Joe Coffey, a graduate of our first Centurions Program class, apply the biblical worldview principles we teach at BreakPoint and the Colson Center. In this marvelous little book, Joe simply and succinctly lays out the tenets of the Christian faith within the context of the four key life and worldview questions. This is an excellent resource for Christians and non-Christians alike who are seeking the Truth."

> ***Chuck Colson, Founder of Prison Fellowship and the Colson Center for Christian Worldview***

"This book may be the best resource I've seen to answer common objections in everyday language."

> ***Jared Totten, Critical Thinking Blog***

"A quick read that packs a punch.... I'm always on the lookout for something like this. *Smooth Stones* is a winner."

> ***Mike del Rosario, ApologeticsGuy.Com***

"Most books on apologetics are too long, too deep, and too complicated. This book has none of these defects. Like its title, it is like a smooth stone from David's apologetic sling directed right to the mind of an enquiring reader."

> ***Norman L. Geisler, Distinguished Professor of Apologetics, Veritas Evangelical Seminary, Murrieta, CA***

Friends and Lovers
Cultivating Companionship and
Intimacy in Marriage

by Joel R. Beeke

**Marriage is for God's glory and our
good.**

The secret?

**Intimate Christian
companionship.**

"A book about love, marriage, and sex from Joel Beeke that is surprisingly candid yet without a trace of smuttiness. Fresh and refreshingly straightforward, this is the best book of its kind."
Derek W H Thomas, Visiting Professor, Reformed Theo. Sem.

"Marriage is hard work. And wonderful. And sometimes, it's both at the same time. *Friends and Lovers* is like a personal mentoring session on marriage with a man whose heart is devoted to seeing Christ honored in how we love each other as husbands and wives. It's full of practical wisdom and grace. A delight."
Bob Lepine, Co-Host, FamilyLife Today

"By laying the theological, emotional, social, and spiritual foundations of marriage before heading to the bedroom, Joel Beeke provides a healthy corrective to the excessive and obsessive sex-focus of our generation and even of some pastors. But, thankfully, he also goes on to provide wise, practical, down-to-earth direction for couples wanting to discover or recover physical intimacy that will both satisfy themselves and honor God."
Dr. David Murray, Professor, Puritan Reformed Theo. Sem.

"There is no better book than this to renew the affection of happy marriage."
Geoffrey Thomas, Pastor, Alfred Place Baptist Church, Wales

Reclaiming Adoption
Missional Living Through the
Rediscovery of Abba Father

Dan Cruver, Editor
John Piper, Scotty Smith
Richard D. Phillips, Jason Kovacs

"There is no greater need in our day
than theological clarity. Dan has
brought us near to God's heart. As
you read this book, you will sense
the need to embrace your own
acceptance as God's adopted child."
–Darrin Patrick, pastor and author

"I can't recall ever hearing about, much less reading, a book like
this before. Simply put, this remarkable volume fills a much-
needed gap in our understanding of what the Bible says both
about God's adoption of us and our adoption of others. I highly
recommend it."
**Sam Storms, author of The Singing God: Discover the Joy
of Being Enjoyed by God**

"The authors writing here are some of the most fearless thinkers and
activists in the Christian orphan care movement. Read. Be empow-
ered. And then join Jesus for the orphans of the world."
Russell D. Moore, pastor and author of Adopted for Life

"With spiritual insight and effective teaching, *Reclaiming Adoption* will help believers better understand our place with Christ
and work in his kingdom."
Ed Stetzer, President, LifeWay Research

"Something like...a revival, is happening right now in evangelical
theology....it may have the momentum to reinvigorate evangelical
systematic theology....The most promising sign I've seen so far is the
new book *Reclaiming Adoption*."
Fred Sanders, Ph.D., Biola University

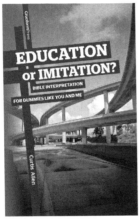

Education or Imitation?

Bible Interpretation for Dummies
Like You and Me

by Curtis Allen

**How can we interpret Scripture
rightly?**

**It's less about education
and more about imitation.**

Imitate Jesus.

"Gritty. Real. Straight. That's what you'll find in Curt Allen's treatment
of Bible interpretation, *Education or Imitation?* And that's what we
need because airy, heady, abstract works on Bible interpretation fail
to do the one thing they're written for—to teach and inspire us to read,
interpret, and apply the Bible. If you want it straight, read this book."

> **Thabiti Anyabwile, author; Senior Pastor, First Baptist Church,
> Grand Cayman; Council Member, The Gospel Coalition**

"Curt Allen's book on interpreting the Bible is wonderfully practical
and clear, giving believers basic principles for understanding God's
Word. He rightly emphasizes that every believer can understand
the Bible. It isn't necessary to be a scholar or preacher or to know
Greek and Hebrew to grasp the Scriptures. Certainly, we are helped
by teachers and scholars, but we can understand the Bible ourselves
and need to test whatever others say by the Scriptures. Allen also
shows that the Bible is Christ-centered. We are only reading the Bible
rightly if we are seeing Jesus Christ, our crucified and risen Lord, in its
pages. At the same time, the Bible is not just meant to be understood
but to be lived out in our everyday lives. I recommend gladly such
an accessible, Christ-centered, and practical book on interpreting the
Scriptures."

> **Thomas R. Schreiner, Professor of New Testament Interpretation,
> The Southern Baptist Theological Seminary**

The Two Fears
Tremble Before God Alone

by Chris Poblete

**You can fear God...
or everything else.**

**Only one fear brings life and hope,
wisdom and joy.**

Fear wisely.

"We are too scared. And we aren't scared enough. Reading this book
will prompt you to seek in your own life the biblical tension between
'fear not' and 'fear God.'"
> ***Russell D. Moore, Dean, Southern Baptist Theological Seminary***

"An importantly counter-cultural book, moving us beyond a
homeboy God we could fist-bump to a holy God we can worship.
The Two Fears helps us recover a biblical fear of God and all the awe,
repentance, and freedom from self-centered fears that go with it. An
awesome resource!"
> ***Dr. Thaddeus Williams, professor, Biola University***

"In this practical and very readable book, Chris Poblete shows how
both the absence of true fear and the presence of 'unholy [false] fear'
stem from an absence of a knowledge of the awesome God of the
Bible, and that, in meeting him, we discover the real dimensions of
creational existence and the wonderful benefits of living in fear and
deep respect before him, freed from the '[false] fear of men.'"
> ***Peter Jones, Ph.D., TruthXchange; Scholar-in-Residence and
> Adjunct Professor, Westminster Seminary in California***

"I commend this book to you: it will fuel your worship and empower
your discipleship."
> ***Gabe Tribbett, Christ's Covenant Church, Winona Lake, IA***

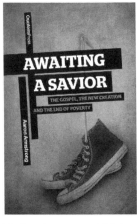

Awaiting a Savior
The Gospel, the New Creation and the End of Poverty

by Aaron Armstrong

Christians are called to serve the poor generously, joyfully, by grace, to the glory of God.

But eliminating poverty is a misguided and dangerous goal.

Poverty is rooted in the fall of man, and there is only one Savior.

"Challenging our own idolatry, our own motivations, and our own actions, *Awaiting a Savior* reorients our mercy ministry around the gospel, seeking to show how a life of love is the overflow of a grace-filled heart."
Trevin Wax, author, editor at Lifeway Christian Resources

"Aaron Armstrong is rightly pessimistic about humanistic solutions, brightly optimistic about God's ultimate solution, and practically realistic about the best and most the Church can do in this present age."
Dr. David P. Murray, Puritan Reformed Theological Seminary

"*Awaiting a Savior* gets at the real but often overlooked cause of poverty. It is a solid theological treatment of what poverty really stems from and how to see it within a biblical framework."
Pastor Dave Kraft, Mars Hill Church, Orange County, author

"Finally, a book that tackles the subject of poverty in a biblical, balanced, thought-provoking, and convicting manner! Walks the fine line of calling for a biblical solution to poverty without causing the reader to feel overly burdened with unnecessary, unbiblical guilt. Aaron also shows how biblical generosity is ultimately rooted in the generosity of God himself."
Stephen Altrogge, pastor, author, TheBlazingCenter.com

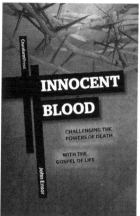

Innocent Blood

Challenging the Powers of Death
with the Gospel of Life

John Ensor

The shedding of innocent blood, primarily through abortion, has now marked an entire generation. But God's call to protect the innocent is unchanged. *We can obey that call.*

"God's Word tells us to be prepared to give an answer to everyone who asks us a reason for the hope within us, and it also tells us that we should do this with gentleness and respect. This book does just that. With decades of experience and true wisdom, John Ensor beautifully shows us how our glorious God delights in our courageous fight for the innocent, and that he commands us to fight, not with the words and weapons of man but with the living and active Gospel of Jesus Christ."

Burk Parsons, pastor; editor of Tabletalk

"...a powerful indictment. There are areas of theology about which sincere Christians can disagree, but this is not one of them."

John Frame, Professor, Reformed Theological Seminary

"By showing how our activism is to be motivated and fueled by the gospel, Ensor challenges us to devote our lives to magnifying Jesus Christ through seeking justice for the unborn."

Trevin Wax, author, editor at LifeWay Christian Resources

"Stellar! John Ensor provides a bridge between the defense of innocent human life and the proclamation of the gospel. His concisely worded thesis is theologically grounded and philosophically sound. I wholeheartedly recommend this book!"

Scott Klusendorf, speaker and author

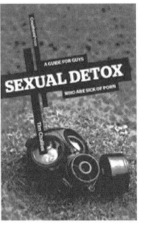

Sexual Detox
A Guide for Guys Who Are Sick of Porn

by Tim Challies

"In an age when sex is worshiped as a god, a little book like this can go a long way to helping men overcome sexual addiction."
   –Pastor Mark Driscoll, Mars Hill Church

"Online pornography is not just a problem for Christian men; it is THE problem. Many men, young and old, in our churches need *Sexual Detox*. Challies offers practical, doable and, above all, gospel-centered hope for men. I want every man I serve and all the guys on our staff to read this book."
   ***Tedd Tripp, pastor, and author of* Shepherding a Child's Heart**

"Tim Challies strikes just the right balance in this necessary work. His assessment of the sexual epidemic in our culture is sober but not without hope. His advice is practical but avoids a checklist mentality. His discussion of sexual sin is frank without being inappropriate. This book will be a valuable resource."
   Kevin DeYoung, pastor and author

"Thank God for using Tim to articulate simply and unashamedly the truth about sex amidst a culture of permissiveness."
   Ben Zobrist, Tampa Bay Rays

"*Sexual Detox* is just what we need. It is clear, honest, and biblical, written with a tone that is knowing but kind, exhortative but gracious, realistic but determined. We have been given by Tim Challies a terrific resource for fighting sin and exalting Christ."
   Owen Strachan, Boyce College

Licensed to Kill
A Field Manual for Mortifying Sin

by Brian G. Hedges

**Your soul is a war zone.
Know your enemy.
Learn to fight.**

"A faithful, smart, Word-centered
guide."
   – *Wes Ward, Revive Our Hearts*

"Are there things you hate that you end up doing anyway? Have you
tried to stop sinning in certain areas of your life, only to face defeat
over and over again? If you're ready to get serious about sin patterns
in your life—ready to put sin to death instead of trying to manage
it—this book outlines the only strategy that works. This is a book I will
return to and regularly recommend to others."
   ***Bob Lepine, Co-Host,* FamilyLife Today**

"Brian Hedges shows the importance of fighting the sin that so easily
entangles us and robs us of our freedom, by fleeing to the finished
work of Christ every day. Well done!"
   ***Tullian Tchividjian, Coral Ridge Presbyterian Church; author,*
   Jesus + Nothing = Everything**

"Rather than aiming at simple moral reformation, *Licensed to Kill* aims
at our spiritual transformation. Like any good field manual, this one
focuses on the most critical information regarding our enemy, and
gives practical instruction concerning the stalking and killing of sin.
This is a theologically solid and helpfully illustrated book that holds
out the gospel confidence of sin's ultimate demise."
   ***Joe Thorn, pastor and author,* Note to Self: The Discipline of
   Preaching to Yourself**

Cruciform
Living the Cross-Shaped Life

by Jimmy Davis

This is the shape of the gospel.

"Jimmy Davis loves the cross. This little book will open your heart up to see how the cross is the center of all of life. Well done."
 — Paul Miller, Director of seeJesus.net, author of *A Praying Life*

"Jimmy Davis shows us how to cut through the fog of contemporary Christian thinking to recover the Savior's plan for our lives."
 T. M. Moore, Dean, Chuck Colson's Centurions Program

"Jimmy shows from personal experience how a lack of passion and purpose, focus and fervor, compassion and conviction, is always due to distance from the now-power of the gospel. I pray that through this book you will rediscover the beauty and brilliance of the gospel in brand new ways."
 Tullian Tchividjian, Coral Ridge Presbyterian Church

"*Cruciform* is a theologically grounded and redemptively freeing picture of a life spent boasting in the cross of Jesus."
 Scotty Smith, Christ Community Church

"This book will be a help to everyone struggling with 'Why, God?' I believe every person planning for, and serving, in a place of Christian ministry should read this book."
 Dr. Brian Richardson, Southern Baptist Theological Seminary

"This is a terrific book for those breakfast discipleship groups. It is the next one I am going to use."
 Dr. William E. Brown, President, Cedarville University

Servanthood as Worship
The Privilege of Life in a Local Church

by Nate Palmer

We [serve] because he first [served] us. - 1 John 1:19 [sort of]

What ever happened to servant-hood? Here is a biblical presenta-tion of our calling to serve in the church, motivated by the grace that is ours in the gospel.

"In an age where the church can be likened to Cinderella—beautiful, but largely ignored and forgotten—Nate Palmer's brief book forces us to rethink both the church and our relationship to her. In an age where egocentrism ensures we sing, 'O say, can you see—what's in it for me?' on a weekly basis, Palmer forces us to say instead, 'How can I best serve the church?' Looking at the needs of others rather than one's own is possibly the most serious deficiency in the church today. Reading this book will help redress the deficiency. I heartily recommend it."

> **Derek W.H. Thomas, *Professor of Theology, Reformed Theological Seminary (Jackson)***

"Think of these pages as a handbook. It contains a sustainable, practical vision for serving in the local church that is powered by grace. Along the way, you'll get a mini theological education."

> ***Justin Buzzard, pastor, San Francisco Bay Area, Buzzard Blog***

"In our media-crazed, me-first culture, the art of the basin and the towel has been shoved off onto those who get paid to serve—certainly a call to serve in humility can't be God's will for all of us, or could it? Nate Palmer gets at the heart of our resistance.. I strongly recommend this book."

> ***Elyse Fitzpatrick, author of* Because He Loves Me**

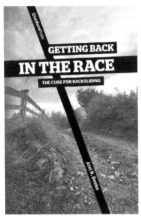

Getting Back in the Race
The Cure for Backsliding

by Joel R. Beeke

Backsliding is the worst thing that can happen to anyone claiming faith in Jesus.

Find out why. Learn the diagnosis. Experience the cure.

"This book is a masterpiece, and I do not say that lightly. This excellent work, so helpfully spiced with quotations from the Puritans, needs to be read over and over again. I heartily commend it."
Martin Holdt, pastor; editor, **Reformation Africa South**

"Joel Beeke's characteristic clarity, biblical fidelity, and unflinching care as to detail and pastoral wisdom is obvious on every page. This book is an honest and sometimes chilling exposition of the seriousness of backsliding; at the same time, it unfailingly breathes the air of grace and hope. Timely and judicious."
Derek W. H. Thomas, First Presbyterian Church, Columbia, SC; Editorial Director, Alliance of Confessing Evangelicals

"'Don't settle for being a spiritual shrimp,' argues Dr. Beeke. The pity is that too many modern Christians are opting for shrimpishly small degrees of grace. Indwelling sin drags the careless believer down into guilty backsliding. This book is a prescription for the believer who feels his guilt."
Maurice Roberts, former editor, **Banner of Truth** *magazine*

"Dr. Beeke outlines the best means of bringing balm and healing to the backslidden soul. Highly recommended."
Michael Haykin, Professor, Southern Baptist Theo. Sem.

Killing Calvinism
How to Destroy a Perfectly Good
Theology from the Inside

by Greg Dutcher

**A resurgence of Calvinism is
changing lives, transforming
churches, and spreading the
gospel. Will it continue or will we
destroy it?**

**That depends on how we live the
message.**

"Brilliant corrective work and I couldn't be more glad he wrote it."
   Matt Chandler, The Village Church; President, Acts 29

"When this kind of critique and warning come from within a movement, it is a sign of health."
   John Piper, Desiring God

"This book blew me away! Greg Dutcher skillfully diagnoses how I kill
the very truth I love by my hypocrisy, pride, anger, and judgmental
attitude. This book will serve a young generation of Calvinists. But
the older generation had better heed it, too. There's medicine here
for all our hearts."
   ***Thabiti Anyabwile, author; Senior Pastor, First Baptist Church,
   Grand Cayman; Council Member, The Gospel Coalition***

"'Dutcher's wisdom will go a long way in bringing spiritual health to
the young, restless, and reformed."
   Sam Storms, Bridgeway Church, Oklahoma City

"An absolute must-read for every YRR—and older Calvinists too! With
wit, compassion, and candor, Greg Dutcher exposes how sin taints
our theological convictions... he shows us Calvinism done right to
the glory of God."
   Lydia Brownback, author and speaker

JOY!

A Bible Study on Philippians for Women

by Keri Folmar

One of the few truly inductive Bible studies intended for use by women. This material has been prepared, and taught, by a pastor's wife in Dubai who previously served as staff attorney for a subcommittee of the U.S. House of Representatives.

"This study points the way into the biblical text, offering a clear and effective guide in studying Paul's letter to the Philippian church. Keri Folmar encourages her readers first and foremost to listen well to God's inspired Word."

> *Kathleen Nielson, author of the* **Living Word Bible Studies;** *Director of Women's Initiatives, The Gospel Coalition*

"Keri's Bible study will not only bring the truths of Philippians to bear upon your life, but will also train you up for better, more effective study of any book of the Bible with her consistent use of the three questions needed in all good Bible study: Observation, Interpretation, and Application."

> *Connie Dever, author of* **The Praise Factory** *children's ministry curriculum and wife of Pastor Mark Dever, President of 9 Marks Ministries*

"'Keri lets the Scriptures do the talking! No cleverly invented stories, ancillary anecdotes, or emotional manipulation here. Keri takes us deeper into the text, deeper into the heart of Paul, deeper into the mind of Christ, and deeper into our own hearts as we pursue Christ for joy in all things. I highly commend this study for your pursuit of joy."

> *Kristie Anyabwile is a graduate of NC State University and wife of Thabiti, a pastor and Gospel Coalition Council Member*

Made in the USA
San Bernardino, CA
26 August 2013